THE POLITICS OF EDUCATION

THE POLITICS OF EDUCATION
Culture, Power, and Liberation

PAULO FREIRE

introduction by Henry A. Giroux

translated by Donaldo Macedo

BERGIN & GARVEY PUBLISHERS, INC.
Massachusetts

Library of Congress Cataloging in Publication Data

Freire, Paulo, 1921–
 The politics of education.

 Includes index.
  1. Literacy. 2. Education—Political aspects.
 3. Education—Social aspects. I. Title.
 LC149.F76 1985   370   84-18572
 ISBN 0-89789-042-6
 ISBN 0-89789-043-4 (pbk.)

First published in 1985 by
Bergin & Garvey Publishers, Inc.
670 Amherst Road
South Hadley, Massachusetts 01075

56789   987654321

Printed in the United States of America

Contents

Translator's Preface

A central theme in Paulo Freire's work is his insistence on the need for readers to adopt a critical attitude when reading a text. That is, readers should critically evaluate the text and not passively accept what is said just because the author said it. Readers must always be prepared to question and to doubt what they have read.

Though I have long been inspired by Freire's challenge, I must admit that I did not so profoundly understand the significance of his insistence that readers be critical and predisposed to question and doubt until I confronted the many dimensions of Freire's thought while translating the contents of this book. To avoid committing serious and unforgivable translation errors and distorting his brilliant and forceful ideas, I was forced to meticulously read and reread each word, each sentence, and each paragraph, in order to engage in a deeper dialogue with the author through his book. I had to understand deeply and experience his concepts in order to render them into English, preserving the same force without sacrificing the music and the poetry of his eloquent prose. This has been a far from easy task. As Edwin and Willa Muir remind us,

> doing a job of translation was like breaking stones, but of course I was wrong to say so. Translating a foreign language into one's language is as fatiguing as breaking stones, but there the resemblance ceases. One is not dealing with blocks of words that have to be trimmed into other shapes; one is struggling with something at once more recalcitrant and more fluid. The spirit of a language, which makes thought flow into molds that are quite different from those of one's native speech. The very shape of thought has to be changed in translation, and that seems to me more difficult than rendering words and idioms into their equivalents."[1]

The translator must be given the freedom to recreate, as Chukovsky succintly pointed out: "The most important thing for the translator to achieve is to recreate in his version of the text the thoughts of the translated author, his 'face,' his 'voice'. . . ."[2] With the help of many friends, particularly Paulo Freire himself, Henry Giroux, and Jack Kimball, I have tried to re-create the author's voice.

The translation of this book posed a constant and provocative challenge; how to preserve the force of Freire's thoughts, in English, while maintaining the fluidity of his writing. In cases where thought was pitted against form, I opted for the former. This is particularly true of terms that are not readily translated into English—terms like *mechanicist* and *technicist*. As originally used, these terms mean more than "mechanical" and "technical," respectively. They embody an ideology with underlying interests that legitimize specific forms of social relations. In our discussions about the translation, Freire insisted that unless North American readers begin to accept the coinage of foreign words in English just as other languages readily incorporate English terms, they will develop a form of linguistic colonialism.

There were other terms that I could only give a close approximation of in the English translation and still others that were untranslatable. A definition of these terms is in order.

The *asentamiento* is an economic organization of agricultural production adopted as an experiment in Chile, and probably in other countries, during the period of agrarian reform. In these organizations the property belongs to the community, and the management of the production process is controlled by the peasants. A *culture circle* is a group of individuals involved in learning to read and write, as well as in the political analysis of their immediate reality and the national interests. In culture circles, reading demands more than decodification of linguistic symbols. It is viewed as a social and political "reading" of the world. The *central team* refers to coordinators responsible for literacy and other activities of culture circles. *Latifundium* is a Spanish and Portuguese word of Latin origin and means a large, privately owned landholding.

This translation would not have been possible without the generous cooperation of many friends. I am grateful to my colleagues at the University of Massachusetts-Boston, particularly Mary Anne Ferguson, Neal Bruss, Gilman Hebert, and Vivian Zamel, who provide me with a stimulating environment and support highly conducive to academic pursuits. I would like to thank my friend and mentor, Henry Giroux, for his guidance and, above all, his faith in me. My thanks also go to Jack

Kimball, a poet, who understood the importance of preserving the force of Freire's thought in English without sacrificing to any great degree the poetry of his prose. Without him, many obstacles that I faced in the course of this translation would have been difficult to overcome. I would also like to express my gratitude to Dale Koike for her careful reading of the manuscript and her invaluable comments and support. Last, but not least, I would like to express my appreciation to my family for their patience and enthusiastic support.

Donaldo P. Macedo
University of Massachusetts
at Boston

NOTES

[1]Edwin and Willa Muir, "Translating from the German," in *On Translation*, (ed.) Reuben A. Brower (Cambridge, Mass.: Harvard University Press, 1959).

[2]Kornei Chukovsky, *A Noble Art* [Vysokoe iskusstvo] (Moscow: Gosudarstvennoe Izdatel'stvo "Khudozhestvennaia Literatura," 1941).

Introduction
by HENRY A. GIROUX

P aulo Freire's newest book appears at an important time for education. In the United States schools have become the subject of an intense national debate forged in a discourse that joins conservatives and radicals alike in their denunciation of public schools and American education. While specific criticisms differ among the diverse ideological positions, the critics share a discourse steeped in the language of crisis and critique. For conservatives, the language of crisis and critique becomes clear in their assertion that schools have failed to take seriously their alleged commitment to the demands of capitalist rationality and the imperatives of the market economy. The crisis pointed to in this case resides in the lagging state of the American economy and the diminishing role of the United States in shaping world affairs. Many on the radical left, by contrast, write off schools as simply a reflex of the labor market. As reproductive sites that smoothly provide the knowledge, skills, and social relations necessary for the functioning of the capitalist economy and dominant society, public education no longer provides the tools for critical thinking and transformative action. Like the work place and the realm of mass culture, schools have become a device for economic and cultural reproduction. Within these contrasting positions, the language of crisis and critique has collapsed into either the discourse of domination or the discourse of despair.

Paulo Freire's newest work represents a theoretically refreshing and politically viable alternative to the current impasse in educational theory and practice worldwide. Freire has appropriated the unclaimed heritage of emancipatory ideas in those versions of secular and religious philosophy located within the corpus of bourgeois thought. He has also critically integrated into his work a heritage of radical thought without assimilating many of the problems that have plagued it historically. In effect, Freire has combined what I call the language of critique with the language of possibility.

Utilizing the language of critique, Freire has fashioned a theory of education that takes seriously the relationship between radical critical theory and the imperatives of radical commitment and struggle. By drawing upon his experiences in Latin America, Africa, and North America, he has generated a discourse that deepens our understanding of the dynamics and complexity of domination. In this instance, Freire has rightly argued that domination cannot be reduced exclusively to a form of class domination. With the notion of difference as a guiding theoretical thread, Freire rejects the idea that there is a universalized form of oppression. Instead, he acknowledges and locates within different social fields forms of suffering that speak to particular modes of domination and, consequently, diverse forms of collective struggle and resistance. By recognizing that certain forms of oppression are not reducible to class oppression, Freire steps outside standard Marxist analyses by arguing that society contains a multiplicity of social relations, which contain contradictions and can serve as a basis from which social groups can struggle and organize themselves. This becomes clear in those social relations in which the ideological and material conditions of gender, racial, and age discrimination are at work.

Equally important is the insight that domination is more than the simple imposition of arbitrary power by one group over another. Instead, for Freire, the logic of domination represents a combination of historical and contemporary ideological and material practices that are never completely successful, always embody contradictions, and are constantly being fought over within asymmetrical relations of power. Underlying Freire's language of critique, in this case, is the insight that history is never foreclosed and that just as the actions of men and women are limited by the specific constraints in which they find themselves, they also make those constraints and the possibilities that may follow from challenging them. It is within this theoretical juncture that Freire introduces a new dimension to radical educational theory and practice. I say it is new because he links the process of struggle to the particularities

of people's lives while simultaneously arguing for a faith in the power
of the oppressed to struggle in the interests of their own liberation. This
is a notion of education fashioned in more than critique and Orwellian
pessimism; it is a discourse that creates a new starting point by trying
to make hope realizable and despair unconvincing.

Education in Freire's view becomes both an ideal and a referent
for change in the service of a new kind of society. As an ideal, education
"speaks" to a form of cultural politics that transcends the theoretical
boundaries of any one specific political doctrine, while also linking social
theory and practice to the deepest aspects of emancipation. Thus, as an
expression of radical social theory, Freire's cultural politics is broader
and more fundamental than any one specific political discourse such as
classical Marxist theory, a point that often confuses his critics. In fact,
his cultural politics represents a theoretical discourse whose underlying
interests are fashioned around a struggle against all forms of subjective
and objective domination as well as a struggle for forms of knowledge,
skills, and social relations that provide the conditions for social and,
hence, self-emancipation.

As a referent for change, education represents both a place within
and a particular type of engagement with the dominant society. For
Freire, education includes and moves beyond the notion of schooling.
Schools represent only one important site where education takes place,
where men and women both produce and are the product of specific
social and pedagogical relations. Education represents in Freire's view
both a struggle for meaning and a struggle over power relations. Its
dynamic is forged in the dialectical relation between individuals and
groups who live out their lives within specific historical conditions
and structural constraints, on the one hand, and those cultural forms
and ideologies that give rise to the contradictions and struggles that
define the lived realities of various societies, on the other. Education is
that terrain where power and politics are given a fundamental expression,
since it is where meaning, desire, language, and values engage and
respond to the deeper beliefs about the very nature of what it means to
be human, to dream, and to name and struggle for a particular future
and way of life. As a referent for change, education represents a form
of action that emerges from a joining of the languages of critique and
possibility. It represents the need for a passionate commitment by educators to make the political more pedagogical, that is, to make critical
reflection and action a fundamental part of a social project that not only

engages forms of oppression but also develops a deep and abiding faith in the struggle to humanize life itself. It is the particular nature of this social project that gives Freire's work its theoretical distinction.

The theoretical distinction of this book can best be understood by examining briefly how Freire's discourse stands between two radical traditions. On the one hand, the language of critique as it is expressed in Freire's work embodies many of the analyses that characterize what has been called the new sociology of education. On the other hand, Freire's philosophy of hope and struggle is rooted in a language of possibility that draws extensively from the tradition of liberation theology. It is from the merging of these two traditions that Freire has produced a discourse that not only gives meaning and theoretical coherence to his work but also provides the basis for a more comprehensive and critical theory of pedagogical struggle.

The New Sociology of Education and the Language of Critique

The new sociology of education emerged in full strength in England and the United States in the early 1970s as a critical response to what can be loosely called the discourse of traditional educational theory and practice. The central question through which it developed its criticism of traditional schooling as well as its own theoretical discourse was typically Freirian: how does one make education meaningful in a way that makes it critical and, hopefully, emancipatory.

Radical critics, for the most part, agreed that educational traditionalists generally ignored the question, and avoided the issue through the paradoxical attempt of depoliticizing the language of schooling while reproducing and legitimating capitalist ideologies. The most obvious expression of this approach could be seen in the positivist discourse used by traditional educational theorists. A positivist discourse, in this case, took as its most important concern the mastery of pedagogical techniques and the transmission of knowledge instrumental to the existing society. In the traditional world view, schools were considered merely instructional sites. That schools were also cultural and political sites was ignored, as was the notion that they represented areas of contention among differently empowered cultural and economic groups.

In the discourse of the new sociology of education, traditional educational theory suppressed important questions about the relations among knowledge, power, and domination. Furthermore, out of this criticism emerged a new theoretical language and mode of criticism that argued that schools did not provide opportunities in the broad Western humanist tradition for self and social empowerment in the society at large. On the contrary, left critics provided theoretical arguments and enormous amounts of empirical evidence to suggest that schools were, in fact, agencies of social, economic, and cultural reproduction. At best, public schooling offered limited individual mobility to members of the working class and other oppressed groups, and in the final analysis they were powerful instruments for the reproduction of capitalist relations of production and the legitimating ideologies of everyday life.

Radical critics within the new sociology of education provided a variety of useful models of analysis to challenge traditional educational ideology. Against the conservative insistence that schools transmitted objective knowledge, radical critics developed theories of the hidden curriculum as well as theories of ideology that identified the interests underlying specific forms of knowledge. Rather than viewing school knowledge as objective, as something to be merely transmitted to students, proponents of the new sociology of education argued that school knowledge was a particular representation of the dominant culture, one that was constructed through a selective process of emphases and exclusions. Against the claim that schools were only instructional sites, radical critics pointed to the transmission and reproduction of a dominant culture in schools, with its selective ordering and privileging of specific forms of language, modes of reasoning, social relations, and cultural forms and experiences. In this view, culture was linked to power and to the imposition of a specific set of ruling class codes and experiences. Moreover, school culture functioned not only to confirm and privilege students from the dominant classes but also through exclusion and insult to discredit the histories, experiences, and dreams of subordinate groups. Finally, against the assertion made by traditional educators that schools were relatively neutral institutions, radical critics illuminated the way in which the state, through its selective grants, certification policies, and legal powers, shaped school practice in the interest of capitalist rationality.

For the new sociology of education, schools were analyzed primarily within the language of critique and domination. Since schools were viewed primarily as reproductive in nature, left critics failed to provide a programmatic discourse through which contrasting hegemonic practices could be established. The agony of the left in this case was that its language of critique offered no hope for teachers, parents, or students to wage a political struggle within the schools themselves. Consequently, the language of critique was subsumed within the discourse of despair.

While working with Brazilian peasant communities, Freire demonstrated that his work shared a remarkable similarity with some of the major theoretical tenets found in the new sociology of education. By redefining and politicizing the notion of literacy, Freire developed a similar type of critical analysis in which he asserted that traditional forms of education functioned primarily to reify and alienate oppressed groups. Moreover, Freire explored in great depth the reproductive nature of dominant culture and systematically analyzed how it functioned through specific social practices and texts to produce and maintain a "culture of silence" among Brazilian peasants. Though Freire did not use the term *hidden curriculum* as part of his discourse, he demonstrated pedagogical approaches through which groups of learners could decide ideological and material practices, and in the form, content, and selective omissions of these one uncovered the logic of domination and oppression. In addition, Freire linked the selection, discussion, and evaluation of knowledge to the pedagogical processes that provided a context for such activity. In his view, it was impossible to separate one from the other and any viable pedagogical practice had to link radical forms of knowledge with corresponding radical social practices.

The major difference between Freire's work and the new sociology of education is that the latter appeared to start and end with the logic of political, economic, and cultural reproduction, whereas Freire's analysis begins with the process of production, that is, with the various ways in which human beings construct their own voices and validate their contradictory experiences within specific historical settings and constraints. The reproduction of capitalist rationality and other forms of oppression was only one political and theoretical moment in the process of domination, rather than an all-encompassing aspect of human existence. It was something to be decoded, challenged, and transformed, but only within the ongoing discourse, experiences, and histories of the oppressed themselves. In this shift from the discourse of reproduction and critique to the language of possibility and engagement, Freire draws from other traditions and fashions a more comprehensive and radical pedagogy.

Liberation Theology and the Language of Possibility

Central to Freire's politics and pedagogy is a philosophical vision of a liberated humanity. The nature of this vision is rooted in a respect for life and the acknowledgment that the hope and vision of the future that inspire it are not meant to provide consolation for the oppressed as much as to promote ongoing forms of critique and a struggle against objective forces of oppression. By combining the dynamics of critique and collective struggle with a philosophy of hope, Freire has created a language of possibility that is rooted in what he calls a permanent prophetic vision. Underlying this prophetic vision is a faith that, as Dorothee Soelle argues in *Choosing Life*, "makes life present to us and so makes it possible. . . . It is a great 'Yes' to life . . . [one that] presupposes our power to struggle."

Freire's attack against all forms of oppression, his call to link ideology critique with collective action, and the prophetic vision central to his politics are heavily indebted to the spirit and ideological dynamics that have both informed and characterized the theologies of liberation that have emerged primarily from Latin America since the early 1970s. In truly dialectical fashion, Freire has criticized and rescued the radical underside of revolutionary Christianity. As the reader will discover in this book, Freire is a harsh critic of the reactionary church. At the same time, he situates his faith and sense of hope in the God of history and of the oppressed, whose teachings make it impossible, in Freire's words, to "reconcile Christian love with the exploitation of human beings."

Within the discourse of theologies of liberation, Freire fashions a powerful theoretical antidote to the cynicism and despair of many left radical critics. The utopian character of his analysis is concrete in its nature and appeal, and takes as its starting point collective actors in their various historical settings and the particularity of their problems and forms of oppression. It is utopian only in the sense that it refuses to surrender to the risks and dangers that face all challenges to dominant power structures. It is prophetic in that it views the kingdom of God as something to be created on earth but only through a faith in both other human beings and the necessity of permanent struggle. The notion of faith that emerges in Freire's work is informed by the memory of the oppressed, the suffering that must not be allowed to continue, and the need to never forget that the prophetic vision is an ongoing process, a vital aspect of the very nature of human life. In short, by combining the discourses of critique and possibility Freire joins history and theology in order to provide the theoretical basis for a radical pedagogy that combines hope, critical reflection, and collective struggle.

It is at this juncture that the work of Paulo Freire becomes crucial to the development of a radical pedagogy. For in Freire, we find the dialectician of contradictions and emancipation. In Freire's work a discourse is developing that bridges the relationship between agency and structure, a discourse that situates human action in constraints forged in historical and contemporary practices, while also pointing to the spaces, contradictions, and forms of resistance that raise the possibility for social struggle. I will conclude by turning briefly to those theoretical elements in Freire's work that are vital for developing a new language and theoretical foundation for a radical theory of pedagogy, particularly in a North American context.

Two qualifications must be made before I begin. First, as will be made clear in this book, Freire's mode of analysis can no longer be dismissed as irrelevant to a North American context. Critics have argued that his experiences with Brazilian peasants do not translate adequately for educators in the advanced industrial countries of the West. Freire makes it clear through the force of his examples and the variety of pedagogical experiences he provides in this book that the context for his work is international in scope. Not only does he draw on his experiences in Brazil, he also includes pedagogical discussion based on his work in Chile, Africa, and the United States. Furthermore, he takes as the object of his criticism both adult education and the pedagogical practices of the Catholic Church, social workers, and public education. As he has pointed out repeatedly, the object of his analysis and the language he uses is for the oppressed everywhere; his concept of the Third World is *ideological* and *political* rather than merely geographical.

This leads to the second qualification. In order to be true to the spirit of Freire's most profound pedagogical beliefs, it must be stated that he would never argue that his work is meant to be adapted in gridlike fashion to any site or pedagogical context. What Freire does provide is a metalanguage that generates a set of categories and social practices that have to be critically mediated by those who would use them for the insights they might provide in different historical settings and contexts. Freire's work is not meant to offer radical recipes for instant forms of critical pedagogy; rather, it is a series of theoretical signposts that need to be decoded and critically appropriated within the specific contexts in which they might be useful.

Freire and the Discourse of Power

Freire provides one of the most dialectical notions of power in contemporary social theory. Power is viewed as both a negative and positive force; its character is dialectical and its mode of operation is always more than simply repressive. For Freire, power works both on and through people. On the one hand, this means that domination is never so complete that power is experienced exclusively as a negative force. On the other hand, it means that power is at the basis of all forms of behavior in which people resist, struggle, and fight for their image of a better world. In a general sense, Freire's theory of power and his demonstration of its dialectical character serve the important function of broadening the terrain on which it operates. Power, in this instance, is not exhausted in those public and private spheres where governments, ruling classes, and other dominant groups operate. It is more ubiquitous and is expressed in a range of oppositional public spaces and spheres that traditionally have been characterized by the *absence* of power and thus any form of resistance.

Freire's view of power suggests not only an alternative perspective to those radical theorists trapped in the straitjacket of despair and cynicism, it also stresses that there are always cracks, tensions, and contradictions in various social spheres such as schools where power is often exercised as a positive force in the name of resistance. Furthermore, Freire understands that power as a form of domination is not simply something imposed by the state through agencies such as the police, the army, and the courts. Domination is also expressed by the way in which power, technology, and ideology come together to produce forms of knowledge, social relations, and other concrete cultural forms that function to actively silence people. But the subtlety of domination is not exhausted by simply referring to those cultural forms that bear down on the oppressed daily; it is also to be found in the way in which the oppressed internalize and thus participate in their own oppression. This is an important point in Freire's work and indicates the ways in which domination is subjectively experienced through its internalization and sedimentation in the very needs of the personality. What is at work here in Freire's thought is an important attempt to examine the psychically repressive aspects of domination and, hence, the possible internal obstacles to self-knowledge and thus to forms of social and self-emancipation.

Freire's notion of domination and how power works repressively on the psyche broadens the notion of learning to include how the body learns tacitly, how habit translates into sedimented history, and how knowledge itself may block the development of certain subjectivities and ways of experiencing the world. This perception of knowledge is important because it points to a radically different conception of how emancipatory forms of knowledge may be refused by those who could benefit most from them. In this case, the oppressed people's accommodation to the logic of domination may take the form of actively resisting forms of knowledge that pose a challenge to their world view. Rather than being a passive acceptance of domination, this form of knowledge becomes instead an active dynamic of negation, an active refusal to listen, to hear, or to affirm one's possibilities. The pedagogical question that emerges from this view of domination is: how do radical educators assess and address the elements of repression and forgetting at the heart of this type of domination? What accounts for the conditions that sustain an active refusal to know or to learn in the face of knowledge that may challenge the nature of domination itself?

The message that emerges from Freire's pedagogy is relatively clear. If radical educators are to understand the meaning of liberation, they must first be aware of the form that domination takes, the nature of its location, and the problems it poses for those who experience it as both a subjective and objective force. But such a project would be impossible unless one took the historical and cultural particularities, the forms of social life, of subordinate and oppressed groups as a starting point for such analysis. It is to this issue in Freire's work that I will now turn.

Freire's Philosophy of Experience and Cultural Production

One of the most important theoretical elements for a radical pedagogy that Freire provides is his view of experience and cultural production. Freire's notion of culture is at odds with both conservative and progressive positions. In the first instance, he rejects the notion that culture can simply be divided into its high, popular, and low forms, with high culture representing the most advanced heritage of a nation. Culture, in this view, hides the ideologies that legitimate and distribute specific forms of culture as if they were unrelated to ruling-class interests and existing configurations of power. In the second instance, he rejects the notion that the moment of cultural creation rests solely with dominant groups and that these cultural forms harbor merely the seeds of domination. Related to this position, and also rejected by Freire, is the assumption that oppressed groups possess by their very location in the apparatus of domination a progressive and revolutionary culture that simply has to be released from the fetters of ruling-class domination.

For Freire, culture is the representation of lived experiences, material artifacts, and practices forged within the unequal and dialectical relations that different groups establish within a given society at a particular point in historical time. Culture is a form of production whose processes are intimately connected with the structuring of different social formations, particularly those that are related to gender, age, race, and class. It is also a form of production that helps human agents to transform society through their use of language and other material resources. In this case, culture is intimately related to the dynamics of power and produces asymmetries in the ability of individuals and groups to define and achieve their goals. Furthermore, culture is also a terrain of struggle and contradictions, and there is no one culture in the homogeneous sense. On the contrary, there are dominant and subordinate cultures that express different interests and operate from different and unequal terrains of power.

Freire argues for a notion of cultural power that takes as its starting point the social and historical particularities, the problems, sufferings, visions, and acts of resistance, that constitute the cultural forms of subordinate groups. Freire's notion of cultural power has a dual focus as part of his strategy to make the political more pedagogical. First, he argues that educators have to work with the experiences that students, adults, and other learners bring to schools and other educational sites. This means making these experiences in their public and private forms the object of debate and confirmation; it means legitimating such experiences in order to give those who live and move within them a sense of affirmation and to provide the conditions for students and others to display an active voice and presence. The pedagogical experience here becomes an invitation to make visible the languages, dreams, values, and encounters that constitute the lives of those whose histories are often actively silenced. But Freire does more than argue for the legitimation of the culture of the oppressed. He also recognizes that such experiences are contradictory in nature and harbor not only radical potentialities but also the sedimentations of domination. Cultural power takes a twist in this instance and refers to the need to *work on* the experiences that make up the lives of the oppressed. This means that such experiences in their varied cultural forms have to be recovered critically in order to reveal both their strengths and weaknesses. Moreover, this means that self-critique is complimented in the name of a radical pedagogy designed to unearth and critically appropriate those unclaimed emancipatory moments in bourgeois knowledge and experience that further provide the skills the oppressed will need to exercise leadership in the dominant society.

What is striking in this view is that Freire has fashioned a theory of cultural power and production that begins with the notion of popular education. Instead of beginning with abstract generalities about human nature, he rightly argues for pedagogical principles that arise from the concrete practices that constitute the terrains on which people live out their problems, hopes, and everyday experiences. All of this suggests taking seriously the cultural capital of the oppressed, developing critical and analytical tools to interrogate it, and staying in touch with dominant definitions of knowledge so we can analyze them for their usefulness and for the ways in which they bear the logic of domination.

Resistant Intellectuals and the Theory-Practice Relationship

Radical social theory has been plagued historically by the relationship between intellectuals and the masses, on the one hand, and the relationship between the forms of theory and practice on which it has been modeled on the other. Under the call for the unity of theory and practice, the possibility for emancipatory practice has often been negated through forms of "vanguardism" in which intellectuals virtually removed from the popular forces the ability to define for themselves the limits of their aims and practice. By assuming a virtual monopoly in the exercise of theoretical leadership, intellectuals unknowingly often reproduced the division of mental and manual labor that was at the core of most forms of domination. Instead of developing theories of practice rooted in the concrete experience of listening and learning with the oppressed, Marxist intellectuals often developed theories for practice, or technical instruments for change, that ignored the necessity for a dialectic reflection on the every day dynamics and problems of the oppressed within the context of radical social transformation.

Freire's work refutes this approach to the theory-practice relationship and redefines the very notion of the intellectual. Like the Italian social theorist Antonio Gramsci, Freire redefines the category of intellectual and argues that all men and women are intellectuals. That is, regardless of one's social and economic function, all human beings perform as intellectuals by constantly interpreting and giving meaning to the world and by participating in a particular conception of the world. Moreover, the oppressed need to develop their own organic and resistant intellectuals who can learn with such groups while simultaneously helping them to foster modes of self-education and struggle against various forms of oppression. In this case, intellectuals are organic in that they are *not* outsiders bringing theory to the masses. On the contrary, they are theorists fused organically with the culture and practical activities of the oppressed. Rather than casually dispense knowledge to the grateful masses, intellectuals fuse with the oppressed in order to make and remake the conditions necessary for a radical social project.

This position is crucially important in highlighting the political function and importance of intellectuals. Equally significant is the way it redefines the notion of political struggle by emphasizing its pedagogical nature and the centrality of the popular and democratic nature of such a struggle. This raises the important question of how Freire defines the relationship between theory and practice.

For Freire, "there is no theoretical context if it is not in a dialectical unity with the concrete context." Rather than call for the collapse of theory into practice, Freire argues for a certain distance between theory and practice. He views theory as anticipatory in its nature and argues that it must take the concepts of understanding and possibility as its central moments. Theory is informed by an oppositional discourse that preserves its critical distance from the "facts" and experiences of the given society. The tension, indeed the conflict with practice, belongs to the essence of theory and is grounded in its very structure. Theory does not dictate practice; rather, it serves to hold practice at arm's length in order to mediate and critically comprehend the type of praxis needed within a specific setting at a particular time in history. There is no appeal to universal laws or historical necessity here; theory emerges from specific contexts and forms of experience in order to examine such contexts critically and then to intervene on the basis of an informed praxis.

But Freire's contribution to the nature of theory and practice and to understanding the role of the intellectual in the process of social transformation contains another important dimension. Freire argues that theory must be seen as the production of forms of discourse that arise from various specific social sites. A discourse may arise from the universities, from peasant communities, from workers' councils, or from various social movements. The issue here is that radical educators recognize that these different sites give rise to various forms of theoretical production and practice. And that each of these sites provides diverse and critical insights into the nature of domination and the possibilities for social and self-emancipation, and they do so from the historical and social particularities that give them meaning. What brings them together is a mutual respect forged in criticism and the need to struggle against all forms of domination.

Freire and the Concept of Historical Insertion

Freire believes that a critical sensibility is an extension of an historical sensibility. That is, to understand the present, in both institutional and social terms, educators must place all pedagogical contexts in an historical context in order to see clearly their genesis and development. History is used by Freire in a twofold sense: on the one hand, it reveals in existing institutions and social relations the historical context that informs their meaning and the legacy that both hides and clarifies their political function. On the other hand, Freire points to the sedimented history that constitutes who we are as historical and social beings. In other words, the history that is anchored in the cultural forms that give meaning to the way we talk, think, dress, and act becomes subject to a form of historical analysis. History in this sense becomes dialectical in Freire's work because it is used to distinguish between the present as given and the present as containing emancipatory possibilities. This perspective makes the present as it constitutes our psyche and the wider society visible in terms of its revolutionary possibilities and in doing so points to the need for a critical awakening (what Freire calls the process of denunciation and annunciation) that is grounded in the capacity for social transformation.

In conclusion, Freire provides in this book a view of pedagogy and praxis that is partisan to its core, for in its origins and intentions it is for "choosing life." Moreover, Freire demonstrates once again that he is not only a man of the present but also a man of the future. His speech, actions, warmth, and vision represent a way of acknowledging and criticizing a world that lives perilously close to destruction. In one sense, Freire's work and presence remind us not simply of what we are but also of the possibilities of what we might become. His newest book could not have come at a more important time.

A Brief Explanation

After considerable hesitation I have finally decided to bring together in one volume recent writings that have not circulated widely, especially in Spanish and English. My basic intention in rewriting and presenting them here is to stimulate more discussion of current major issues in education.

Together with *Extension or Communication*, published in Brazil in 1970 by Paz e Terra, this volume may help fill possible gaps between *Cultural Action for Freedom* and *Pedagogy of the Oppressed*. Finally, I hope that my continually returning to certain themes in different chapters and even in the same chapter will not prove tiresome for the reader. This is, after all, my way of writing about what I think and thinking about what I do.

CHAPTER ONE

The Act of Study

In compiling any bibliography, there is one intrinsic purpose: focusing or stimulating a desire in a potential reader to learn more.[1] If a bibliography does not fulfill this purpose, if it seems to be missing something or does not challenge those who read it, the motive to use it is undermined.

A bibliography then becomes useless, lost among other things in desk drawers.

In developing a bibliography, there are three categories of audience: the people it addresses, the authors cited, and other bibliographic writers in general. A bibliographic list cannot be compiled merely by haphazardly copying titles or through hearsay. Further, a bibliography shouldn't prescribe readings dogmatically; it should offer a challenge to those reading it. This challenge becomes more concrete as one begins studying

1

the works cited, not merely reading superficially or simply scanning pages.

Indeed, studying is a difficult task that requires a systematic critical attitude and intellectual discipline acquired only through practice. This critical attitude is precisely what "banking education" does not engender.[2] Quite the contrary, its focus is fundamentally to kill our curiosity, our inquisitive spirit, and our creativity. A student's discipline becomes a discipline for ingenuity in relation to the text, rather than an essential critique of it.

When readers submit to this ingenuous process, reading becomes purely mechanical and this, among other factors, can explain the readers' tuning out on the text and daydreaming about other things. What is required of readers, in essence, is not comprehension of content but memorization. Instead of understanding the text, the challenge becomes its memorization and if readers can do this, they will have responded to the challenge.

In a critical vision, things happen differently: A reader feels challenged by the entire text and the reader's goal is to appropriate its deeper meaning.

Here are some essential criteria for developing a critical posture in the act of study:

(a) The reader should assume the role of subject of the act. It's impossible to study seriously if the reader faces a text as though magnetized by the author's word, mesmerized by a magical force; if the reader behaves passively and becomes "domesticated," trying only to memorize the author's ideas; if the reader lets himself or herself be "invaded" by what the author affirms; if the reader is transformed into a "vessel" filled by extracts from an internalized text.

Seriously studying a text calls for an analysis of the study of the one who, through studying, wrote it. It requires an understanding of the sociological-historical conditioning of knowledge. And it requires an investigation of the content under study and of other dimensions of knowledge. Studying is a form of reinventing, re–creating, rewriting; and this is a subject's, not an object's, task. Further, with this approach, a reader cannot separate herself or himself from the text because she or he would be renouncing a critical attitude toward the text.

This critical attitude in studying is the same as that required in dealing with the world (that is, the real world and life in general), an attitude of inward questioning through which increasingly one begins to see the reasons behind facts.

We study more thoroughly the more we strive for a global view and apply this to the text, distinguishing its component dimensions. Re-reading a book to determine these demarcations makes the meaning of its global quality more significant.

In delimiting these central issues that in their interaction constitute the unity of the text, the critical reader will be amazed by the matrix of themes not always explicit in the index of a book. Demarcations of these themes, of course, should also incorporate a subject-reader's frame of reference.

When reading a book, we subject-readers should be receptive to any passage that triggers a deeper reflection on any topic, even if it's not the main subject of the book. Sensing a possible relationship between the read passage and our preoccupation, we as good readers should concentrate on analyzing the text, looking for a connection between the main idea and our own interest. Nonetheless, there is a prerequisite: We must analyze the content of the passage, keeping in mind what comes before and after it, in order not to betray the author's total thinking.

Once we establish the relative point between the passage under study and our own interest, we should make a note of it on a file card with a title that identifies it with the specific study topic. We should take our time pondering this passage since a written text offers us this latitude. Later, we can continue reading, concentrating on whatever other passages invite deeper reflection.

In the final analysis, the serious study of a book, like that of an article, implies not merely critical penetration into its basic content but also penetration into an acute sensibility, a permanent intellectual disquiet, a predisposition to investigation.

(b) The act of study, in sum, is an attitude toward the world. Because the act of study is an attitude toward the world, the act of study cannot be reduced to the realtionship of reader to book or reader to text.

In fact, a book reflects its author's confrontation with the world. It expresses this confrontation. And even when an author pays no attention to concrete reality, he or she will be expressing his or her own special way of confronting it. Studying is, above all, thinking about experience, and thinking about experience is the best way to think accurately. One who studies should never stop being curious about other people and reality. There are those who ask, those who try to find answers, and those who keep on searching.

Maintaining this curious attitude helps us to be skillfull and to profit from our curiosity. In this way we use what we have already learned in confronting everyday experience and conversation.

Flashes of ideas that often "assault" us as we walk down the street are, in effect, what Wright Mills calls a file of ideas.[3] These flashes, when filed correctly, are real challenges that we should address. When we transform these flashes into deeper thoughts, they almost always become a means for even deeper reflection while reading a text.

(c) Studying a specific subject calls for us, whenever possible, to be familiar with a given bibliography, in either a general subject or the area of our ongoing inquiry.

(d) The act of study assumes a dialectical relationship between reader and author, whose reflections are found within the themes he treats.

This dialectic involves the author's historical-sociologial and ideological conditioning, which is usually not the same as that of the reader.

(e) The act of study demands a sense of modesty.

If we really assume a modest attitude compatible with a critical attitude, we need not feel foolish when confronted with even great difficulties in trying to discern a deeper meaning from a text. A book isn't always that easy to understand. Modest and critical, we know that a text can often be beyond our immediate ability to respond because it *is* a challenge.

In this case, what we should recognize is the need to be better equipped, and when we are prepared we should return to the text. Indeed, it won't help to go on to the next page if the page we are reading isn't understood. Quite the contrary, we must be committed to unlocking its mysteries. Understanding a text isn't a gift from someone else. It requires patience and commitment from those who find it problematic.

The act of study should not be measured by the number of pages read in one night or the quantity of books read in a semester.

To study is not to consume ideas, but to create and re–create them.

NOTES

1. This essay was written in Chile. It served as the introduction to the bibliography which was proposed to the participants of the National Seminar on Education and Agrarian Reform.

2. On "banking education", see Paulo Freire, *Pedagogy of the Oppressed*.

3. Wright Mills, *The Sociological Imagination*.

CHAPTER TWO

Adult Literacy: The Ingenuous and the Critical Visions

O ur concept of illiteracy is naive, at best, when we compare it, on the one hand, to a "poison herb" (as is implied in the current expression "eradication of illiteracy") and, on the other, to a "disease" that's contagious and transmitted to others.[1] Again, sometimes we see it as a depressing "ulcer" that should be "cured". Its indices, statistically compiled by international organizations, distort the level of "civilization" of certain societies. Moreover, from this ingenuous or astute perspective, illiteracy can also appear as a manifestation of people's "incapacity," their "lack of intelligence," or their proverbial "laziness."

When educators limit their understanding of this complex issue, which they may not appreciate (or not wish to appreciate), their solutions are always of a mechanical character. Literacy, as such, is reduced to the mechanical act of "depositing" words, syllables, and letters *into*

7

illiterates. This "deposit" is sufficient as soon as the illiterate student attaches a magical meaning to the word and thus "affirms" himself or herself.

Written or read, words are, as it were, amulets placed on a person who doesn't say them, but merely repeats them, almost always without any relation to the world and the things they name.

Literacy becomes the result of an act by a so-called educator who "fills" the illiterate learner with words. This magical sense given to words extends to another ingenuity: that of the Messiah. The illiterate is a "lost man." Therefore, one must "save" him, and his "salvation" consists of "being filled" with these words, mere miraculous sounds offered or imposed on him by the teacher who is often an unconscious agent of the political policies inherent in the literacy campaign.

The Texts

From a methodological or sociological point of view, primers developed mechanistically, like any other texts, cannot escape a type of original sin however good they may be, since they are instruments for "depositing" the educator's words into the learners. And since they limit the power of expression and creativity, they are domesticating instruments.

Generally speaking, these texts and primers are developed according to mechanical and magical-Messianic concepts of "word-deposit" and "word-sound." Their ultimate objective is to achieve a "transfusion" in which the educator is the "blood of salvation" for the "diseased illiterate." Moreover, even when the words from which a text is developed coincide with the existential reality of illiterate learners (and this rarely occurs), they are presented as clichés; the words are never created by the ones who should have written them.

Most often these words and texts have nothing to do with the actual experience of illiterate learners. When there is some relationship between the words and the learners' experience, its expression is so contrived and paternalistic that we don't even dare call it infantile.

This way of handling illiterates implies a distorted opinion—it is as if illiterates were totally different from everyone else. This distortion fails to acknowledge their real-life experience and all the past and ongoing knowledge acquired through their experience.

As passive and docile beings (since this is how they are viewed and treated), illiterate learners must continue to receive "transfusions." This is, of course, an alienating experience, incapable of contributing to the process of transformation of reality.

What meaning is there to a text that asks absurd questions and gives equally absurd answers? Consider this example. *Ada deu o dedo ao urubu?* "Did Ada give her finger to urubu?" The author of the question answers, "I doubt that Ada gave her finger to the bird!"

First, we don't know of any place in the world where one invites the *urubu* to land on one's finger. Second, in supplying an answer to his own strange question, the author implicitly doubts that the *urubu* is a bird, since he expects the student to answer that Ada gave her finger to "the bird," rather than "to *urubu*."[2]

What real meaning could texts such as these have for men and women, peasants or urbanites, who spend their day working hard or, even worse, without working. Let us consider these texts, which must be memorized: *A asa é da ave*—"The wing is of the bird"; *Eva viu a uva*—"Eva saw the grape"; *João já sabe ler. Vejam a alegria em sua face. João agora vai conseguir um emprego*—"John already knows how to read. Look at the happiness in his face. Now John will be able to find a job."[3]

These texts are usually illustrated with cute little houses, heart-warming, and well decorated, with smiling couples fair of face (usually white and blond), well-nourished children sporting shoulder bags, waving goodbye to their parents on their way to school after a succulent breakfast.

What positive view can peasants or urban workers gain for their role in the world? How can they critically understand their concrete oppressive situation through literacy work in which they are instructed with sweetness to learn phrases like "the wing of the bird" or "Eva saw the grape"?

By relying on words that transmit an ideology of accommodation, such literacy work reinforces the "culture of silence" that dominates most people. This kind of literacy can never be an instrument for transforming the real world.

The Learners

If this literacy approach does not have the necessary force in itself to fulfill at least *some* of the illusions it transmits to the students (such as the implicit promise in one example that the illiterate who learns to read will now "find a job"), sooner or later this approach will end up working against the soothing objectives of the very system whose ideology it reproduces.

Consider ex-illiterates who were "trained" by reading texts (without, of course, their analyzing what is involved in the social context) and who can read, even though they do so mechanically. When looking for work or better jobs, they can't find them. They, at least, understand the fallacy and impossibility of such a promise.

Critically speaking, illiteracy is neither an "ulcer" nor a "poison herb" to be eradicated, nor a "disease." Illiteracy is one of the concrete expressions of an unjust social reality. Illiteracy is not a strictly linguistic or exclusively pedagogical or methodological problem. It is political, as is the very literacy through which we try to overcome illiteracy. Dwelling naively or astutely on intelligence does not affect in the least the intrinsic politics.

Accordingly, the critical view of literacy does not include the mere mechanical repetition of *pa, pe, pi, po, pu* and *la, le, li, lo, lu* to produce *pula, pêlo, láli, pulo, lapa, lapela, pílula*, and so on. Rather, it develops students' consciousness of their rights, along with their critical presence in the real world. Literacy in this perspective, and not that of the dominant classes, establishes itself as a process of search and creation by which illiterate learners are challenged to perceive the deeper meaning of language and the word, the word that, in essence, they are being denied.

To deny the word implies something more: It implies the denial of the right to "proclaim the world."[4] Thus, to "say a word" does not mean merely repeating any word. Indeed, such repetition constitutes one of the sophisms of reactionary literacy practice.

Learning to read and write cannot be done as something parallel or nearly parallel to the illiterates' reality. Hence, as we have said, the learning process demands an understanding of the deeper meaning of the word.

More than writing and reading "the wing is of the bird," illiterate learners must see the need for another learning process: that of "writing" about one's life, "reading" about one's reality. This is not feasible if learners fail to take history in hand and make it themselves—given that history can be made and remade.

Both the learner and the educator need to develop accurate ways of thinking about reality. And this is achieved, not through repeating phrases that seem to be nonsensical, but by respecting the unity between practice and theory. It is most essential to liberate the equivocal theory by which learners usually become victims linked to verbalism, to nonsensical syllables that are just a waste of time.

This explains such oft-repeated expressions as "You'd have much better results if education were less theoretical and more practical," or "We need to eliminate these theoretical courses."

This also explains the distinction made between theoretical and practical men and women, the former considered to be at the periphery of action while the latter realize it. A distinction should be made, however, between theoreticians and verbalists. Theoreticians then would also be practitioners.

What should be contrasted with practice is not theory, which is inseparable from it, but the nonsense sounds of imitative thinking.

Since we can't link theory with verbalism, we can't link practice with activism. Verbalism lacks action; activism lacks a critical reflection on action.

It's not that strange, then, for verbalists to retreat to their ivory tower and see little merit in those who are committed to action, while activists consider those who conceptualize an act as "noxious intellectuals," "theoreticians," or "philosophers" who do nothing but undercut their work.

For me, I see myself between both groups, among those who won't accept the impossible division between practice and theory, since all educational practice implies an educational theory.

Theory and Practice

The theoretical foundations of my practice are explained in the actual process, not as a *fait accompli*, but as a dynamic movement in which both theory and practice make and remake themselves. Many things that today still appear to me as valid (not only in actual or future practice but also in any theoretical interpretation that I might derive from it) could be outgrown tomorrow, not just by me, but by others as well.

The crux here, I believe, is that I must be constantly open to criticism and sustain my curiosity, always ready for revision based on the results of my future experience and that of others. And in turn, those who put my experience into practice must strive to recreate it and also rethink my thinking. In so doing, they should bear in mind that no educational practice takes place in a vacuum, only in a real context—historical, economic, political, and not necessarily identical to any other context.

A critical view of my experience in Brazil requires an understanding of its context. My practice, while social, did not belong to me. Hence my difficulty in understanding my experience, not to mention in my applying it elsewhere without comprehending the historical climate where it originally took place.

This effort toward understanding, required of me and others, again highlights the unity between practice and theory. But understanding the relationship between practice and theory in education also requires seeing the connection between social theory and practice in a given society. A theory that is supposed to inform the general experience of the dominant classes, of which educational practice is a dimension, can't be the same as one that lends support to the rejustification of the dominant classes in their practice. Thus, educational practice and its theory cannot be neutral. The relationship between practice and theory in an education oriented toward liberation is one thing, but quite another in education for the purpose of "domestication." For example, dominant classes don't need to worry about the unity between practice and theory when they defer (to mention only one example) to so-called skilled labor because here the theory referred to is a "neutral theory" of a "neutral technique."

Adult literacy is now heading toward another alternative.

The first practical requirement that a critical view of literacy imposes is that of generative words.[5] These are the words with which illiterate learners gain their first literacy as subjects of the process, expanding their original "restrictive vocabulary universe." These words incorporate a meaningful thematic of the learners' lives.

The educator can organize a program only through investigating this vocabulary universe; the world defined by the given words. The program in this form comes from the learners and is later returned to them, not as a dissertation, but as a problem or the posing of a problem.

Conversely, through the other kind of practice we discussed earlier, when the educator develops his primer, at least from a sociocultural point of view he arbitrarily selects his generative words from books in his library, a process generally considered valid throughout the world.

In a critical approach, it's most important to select generative words in relation to language levels, including the pragmatic. Further, these words cannot be selected according to purely phonetic criteria. A word can have a special force in one area, for instance, and not in others: This variation in meaning can occur even within the same city.

Let's consider another point. In a mechanical practice of literacy, the primer's author selects words, decomposes these words for the purpose of analysis, and composes them in conjunction with other words with identical syllables; then, using these fabricated words, he writes his texts. In the practice that we defend, generative words—people's words—are used in realistic problem situations ("codifications") as challenges that call for answers from the illiterate learners.[6] "To problematize" the word that comes from people means to problematize the thematic element to which it refers. This necessarily involves an analysis of reality. And reality reveals itself when we go beyond purely sensible knowledge to the reasons behind the factors. Illiterate learners gradually begin to appreciate that, as human beings, to speak is not the same as to "utter a word."

Illiteracy and Literacy

It is essential to see that illiteracy is not in itself the original obstacle. It's the result of an earlier hindrance and later becomes an obstacle. No one elects to be illiterate. One is illiterate because of objective conditions. In certain circumstances "the illiterate man is the man who does not need to read."[7] In other circumstances, he is the one to whom the right to read was denied. In either case, there is no choice.

In the first case the person lives in a culture whose communication and history are, if not always, at least mostly oral. Writing does not bear any meaning here. In a reality like this, to succeed in introducing the written word and with it literacy, one needs to change the situation qualitatively. Many cases of regressive literacy can be explained by the introduction of such changes, the consequence of a Messianic literacy naively conceived for areas whose tradition is preponderantly or totally oral.

From various opportunities I have had to converse with Third World peasants, especially in areas where conflicts arose in their experiments with agrarian reform, I've heard expressions like these: "Before agrarian reform we didn't need letters. First, because we didn't used to think. Our thinking belonged to master. Second, because we didn't have anything to do with letters. Now, things are different." In this case, the person recognizes his or her illiteracy to be the result of objective conditions.

In the second case, by participating in a literate culture, the person who cannot read comes to be considered illiterate. The illiterate in this instance is one who hasn't had the opportunity to become literate.

I'll never forget the description given by a peasant from the Brazilian northeast during a discussion of two codifications that we presented. The first presented an Indian hunting with his bow and arrow; the second, a peasant like himself, also hunting, with a rifle. "Between these two hunters," he asserted, "only the second can be illiterate. The first is not."

"Why?" I asked him. Smiling as if surprised by my question, he answered, "One cannot say that the Indian is illiterate because he lives in a culture that does not recognize letters. To be illiterate you need to live where there are letters and you don't know them."

Truthfully, the illiterate learner can understand this in its deeper sense only when he or she recognizes that his or her own illiteracy is problematical. And this awareness won't come through phrases like "Eva saw the grape" or "the wing of the bird" or "Ada gave her finger to the *urubu*."

Again we emphasize that in the practice we propose, learners begin to perceive reality as a totality; whereas in a reactionary practice learners will not develop themselves, nor can they develop a lucid vision of their reality. They will overuse what we call a focalist vision of reality, by which components are seen without integration in the total composition.

Transformative Literacy

As illiterate learners go on to organize a more precise form of thinking through a problematical vision of their world and a critical analysis of their experience, they will be able increasingly to act with more security in the world.

Literacy then becomes a global task involving illiterate learners in their relationships with the world and with others. But in understanding this global task and based on their social experience, learners contribute to their own ability to take charge as the actors of the task—the praxis. And significantly, as actors they transform the world with their work and create their own world. This world, created by the transformation of another world they did not create and that now restrains them, is the cultured world that stretches out into the world of history.

Similarly, they understand the creative and regenerative meaning of their transformative work. They discover a new meaning as well. For instance, chopping down a tree, cutting it into pieces, and processing the logs according to a plan will create something that is no longer a tree. Thus they come to appreciate that this new thing, a product of their efforts, is a cultural object.

From discovery to discovery, they reach the fundamental truth:

(a) Obstacles to their right to "utter the word" are in direct relationship to the establishment's lack of appreciating them and the product of their work.
(b) Given that their work provides them a certain knowledge, it's not highly significant that they are illiterates.
(c) Finally, human ignorance and knowledge are not absolute. No one knows everything. No one is ignorant of everything.

From my experience in Brazil and from my past practice in Chile, these truths have been continually confirmed.

In discussing the meaning of work, an old Chilean peasant once said, "Now I know that I'm a cultured man." When asked why he felt cultured, he replied, "Because through work and by working I change the world."

This type of affirmation reveals people seeing at a truly practical level that their presence in the world (through a critical response to this presence) is implied by the knowledge that they are not only in the world but *with* the world.

It's an important new awareness when we realize we are cultured because through work and by working we change the world (even though there's a lot to be done between the recognition of this and the real transformation of society). This understanding cannot be compared with the monotonous repetition of *ba, be, bi, bo, bu*.

"I like talking about this," a woman said, also a Chilean, pointing to the codification of her own living situation, "because that's the way I live. But while I am living this way, I don't see it. Now, yes, I can see the way I am living."

Challenged by her own way of living as depicted in the codification, this woman could understand her life in a way she couldn't see before. She did this by an "immersion" in her own existence, by "admiring" it.[8] Making the way she lives obvious in her consciousness, describing it and analyzing it, amount to an unveiling of her reality, if not a political engagement for her transformation.

Recently we had a chance to hear similar statements during a discussion of a neighborhood street scene from a man who lives in New York.

After quietly studying the scene in some detail—trash cans, garbage, other typical aspects of a slum—he suddenly said, "I live here. I walk on these streets every day. I can't say that I ever noticed all this. But now I understand what I didn't used to see."[9] Basically, this New Yorker understood on that night his previous perception. He could correct his distorted view by distancing himself from his reality through its codification.

Correcting one's earlier perception isn't always easy. The relation between subject and object means that revealing an objective reality equally affects its subjective qualities, and sometimes in an intensely dramatic and painful manner.

Under certain circumstances, in a kind of consciousness awakening, instead of accepting reality, one avoids this through wishful thinking, which becomes real. During another discussion group in New York, we were looking over an impressive photomontage of city streets with various kinds of buildings that were representative of different social levels. Though the members of this group were doubtlessly from the lowest rung on the economic ladder, they chose a middle rung when asked to examine the montage and to find their own level.

I have also found this same resistance to accepting reality—a kind of defensiveness—among peasants and urban workers in Latin America. In Chile, during a debate on their new experience in the *asentamiento* ("settlements"), there were those who expressed a certain lingering nostalgia for their old masters as well as others who went on deciphering their reality in critical terms. Conditioned by dominant ideology, those who remain nostalgic not only wipe out their capacity to see their reality, but sometimes they sheepishly submit themselves to the myths of that ideology as well.

Adult literacy, as we understand it, like postliteracy, comprises some crucial elements that must be confronted.

At a time when his relationship to man and world was made problematical, another Chilean peasant claimed, "I see now there isn't any man without the world." The educator asked him one more problematical question. Suppose all human beings were dead, but there were still trees, birds, animals, rivers, the sea, the mountains—would this be a world? "No," he answered emphatically, "someone who could say 'This is the world' would be missing."

Through his response, our philosopher-peasant (an "absolute ignorant" by elitist standards) raised the dialectical question of subjectivity-objectivity.

After two months of participation in cultural discussion group activities, another peasant explained, "When we were tenants and the master would çall us naive, we would say, 'Thank you, Master.' To us, that was a compliment. Now that we're becoming critical, we know what he meant by *naive*. He was calling us fools."[10] We asked him, "What do you mean by becoming critical?" "To think correctly," he answered, "to see reality as it is."

There is one last point to consider. All these oral reactions from cultural discussion groups should be transcribed into texts that are then given back to illiterate learners so that they can begin to discuss them.

This hardly relates to the criticized practice of having learners repeat twice, three times, and memorize "the wing is of the bird."

On the basis of the social experience of illiterates, we can conclude that only a literacy that associates the learning of reading and writing with a creative act will exercise the critical comprehension of that experience, and without any illusion of triggering liberation, it will nevertheless contribute to its process.

And, of course, this is no task for the dominant classes.

NOTES

1. When I say "concept of illiteracy is naive at best," it is because many people who could be considered as "naive", when they express the above concept, they are, in fact, astute. They know very well what they are doing and where they want to go, when, in literacy campaigns, they "feed" the illiterates with alienating slogans under the cover of neutrality of education. Objectively, they identify themselves as both naive and astute.

2. *Urubu* means "vulture" in Portuguese.

3. For additional examples and related discussion, see chap.6.

4. On this subject, see Ernani Maria Fiori, Preface to *Pedagogy of the Oppressed*.

5. For a definition of the term *generative word*, see chap.6, n.2.

6. For a definition of the term *codification*, see chap.6, n.14.

7. Alvaro Vieira Pinto, *Consciência e realidade* (Rio: ISEB, 1960).

8. For a discussion of the term *admiring*, see chap.6.

9. This work was part of the institute called Full Circle, directed by Robert Fox, a Catholic priest. It was a post-literacy program. There is something similar between the work of these educators and the work we did in Brazil and tried to do in Chile. However, we did not have any influence on their concept of education. I met them when I visited their program at the suggestion of Ivan Illich.

CHAPTER THREE

Peasants and Their Reading Texts

To change the world through work, to "proclaim" the world, to express it, and to express oneself are the unique qualities of human beings. Education at any level will be more rewarding if it stimulates the development of this radical, human need for expression.

This is exactly what "banking education" (as I sometimes call it) does not do. In banking education an educator replaces self-expression with a "deposit" that a student is expected to "capitalize." The more efficiently he does this, the better educated he is considered.

In adult literacy, as in postliteracy, mastering oral and written language constitutes one dimension of the process of being expressive. Learning to read and write, then, won't have any meaning if it's done through a purely mechanical repetition of syllables.

This learning process is valid only when the learner begins si-

21

multaneously to perceive the deep structure of language along with mastering the mechanics of vocabulary. When she or he begins to perceive the close relationship between language-thought and reality in her or his own transformation, she or he will see the need for new forms of comprehension and, also, expression.

Such is the case with agrarian reform. Once the latifundium (large estate) system is transformed into *asentamiento* (individual settlements for the former tenants of the large estates), one would expect new forms of expression and of thought-language.

In establishing these settlements, words and whole phrases that used to incorporate cultural constellations and world views typical of the latifundium system tend to lose their original force.

"Master. Yes, master." "What can I do if I am only a peasant?" "Speak and we will follow." "If the master said it, it must be true." "Do you know whom you are talking to?" These words and phrases are incompatible with the concept of the *asentamiento,* since this is a system that democratizes itself. If along with these changes a means of education could be developed to further critical understanding of the political and economic change that has taken place—and has fundamentally transformed work habits, as well—this education would also help establish a new thought-language.

Let it be enough to underscore the idea of the relation between thought-language and social structure, so that adult literacy and post-literacy might have distinct meanings.

The Role of Educators

Mindful of these relationships, educators should pay great attention to selecting generative words when writing reading texts.[1] These texts should address men and women in the context of their transformation. These texts can't be just a description of the new reality, or a mere retelling of a paternalistic theme. One must consider content, form, the potential for other uses, and increasing complexity when developing these texts.

Their objective shouldn't be to describe something to be memorized. Quite the contrary, they should "problematize" situations, present the challenge of reality that the learners confront everyday. These texts must embody a challenge in themselves and as such they should be regarded dialectically by the learners and the educator so that they can delve deeply into the texts' meaning. Texts, of course, should never be reduced to "rhymes" that put one to sleep instead of rousing critical consciousness. Rather than follow typical routines, the "reading classes" should be actual reading seminars with constant opportunity to establish the relation between a passage of a text under discussion and various aspects of the real world of the *asentamiento*.

A word, an affirmation followed up in the text that's being analyzed, can spark a viable discussion around the core issues of the *asentamiento:* adjusting to new conditions, health problems, and the need to develop effective methods of responding to new challenges.

All this requires not only rigorous conviction from base educators but also ongoing evaluation of their own work.

Evaluation, that is, and not inspection. Through inspection, educators just become objects of vigilance by a central organization. Through evaluation, everyone is a subject along with the central organization in the act of criticism and establishing distance from the work.

In understanding the process in this way, evaluation is not an act by which educator A evaluates educator B. It's an act by which educators A and B together evaluate an experience, its development, and the obstacles one confronts along with any mistakes or errors. Thus, evaluation has a dialectical character.

After establishing a sense of distance from action realized, or action that's being realized, the evaluators can examine it. Then, many things not seen in the actual process become obvious.

In a sense, instead of a fiscal tool, evaluation is the presentation of action as problem posing.

It's essential that members of the evaluating organization deeply believe that they have as much to learn from educators directly linked to popular bases as those who study at the bases. Without this attitude, the evaluators from an external organization will never admit to any gap between their view of reality and reality.

If something doesn't go well, it's because of the educators at the base, never the result of a fault in the theory of the evaluators from outside. By believing they possess the truth, the evaluators act out their infallibility. And with such a hypothesis, when they evaluate, they inspect.

Accordingly, the more bureaucratic the evaluators are, not just from an administrative point of view but above all from an intellectual view, the narrower and more inspectionlike the evaluators from outside will be. Conversely, the more open and accessible to creativity they are, the more antidogmatic, and the more evaluative (in the sense here described) they will be.

In addition to the texts developed by outside educators, teachers absolutely must take advantage of the texts written by peasants. Gradually, these should increase in number. But this doesn't mean that outside educators should stop writing texts or stop using texts prepared by specialists (like rural economists or health specialists).

Actually, educators should take advantage of all opportunities to stimulate peasants, even by sharing their own views, doubts, and criticisms.

During a discussion of a problematical situation—like codification—educators should ask peasants to write down their reactions—a simple phrase or whatever—first on the blackboard, and then, on a sheet of paper.

These two periods of writing have distinct objectives. The goal of the first period is to propose a group discussion around the ideas written by one of their peers. In order for the experience to be reinforced, the author should coordinate the discussion.

The purpose of the second period, during which the learner writes his or her thoughts on a sheet of paper, is to develop material for later use in an anthology of peasants' texts. This anthology should be organized jointly by outside educators, base educators, and some peasants as well. Once the texts are selected and classified by themes, the educators could write individual comments, simple and problem posing in character. Another way to collect peasant discourse and convert it into reading texts is to tape-record discussions among groups of peasants.

The "codification" that peasants have in front of them is not a mere visual aid, one that the educator uses to "conduct" a better class.[2] The codification, to the contrary, is an object of knowledge that, in mediating between the educator and students, allows its own unveiling to take place.

By representing an aspect of the peasants' concrete reality, the codification contains the generative word that refers to the codification or to some of its elements.

While participating with the educator in "decodifying" a codification, peasants analyze their reality and in their discourse they express levels of seeing themselves relative to an objective situation.[3] They reveal the ideological conditioning to which they were subjected in the "culture of silence" and in the latifundium system.

For all of us who have participated in projects like this, experience has shown the significance and the richness of illiterates' language in analyzing their reality as depicted in the codification. From whatever angle we address it—be it form or content—this significance and richness involve a linguistic analysis that in turn includes ideology and politics.

This material offers educators a number of possibilities that shouldn't be overlooked. Suggestions we'll make about such possibilities will doubtlessly challenge educators to offer others.

Even before debates on the codifications are transcribed, the first application of this material could be to set up evaluation seminars during which educators could listen to the tapes with one another and discuss their behavior during the decodification process. In the context of the evaluation seminar, the educators would establish distance from their previous experience, gaining insight into their accomplishments and their mistakes. In addition, it would be essential for educators working in area A to listen to tapes of discussions from area B and vice versa.

Similar efforts could be made at the level of illiterate learners. Peasants from area A could listen to and discuss the tape recordings of their peers from area B decodifying the same codifications that they also had codified and vice versa.

An effort such as this would help both learners and educators overcome what I usually call the focalist vision of reality and gain an understanding of the totality.

The Role of Specialists

It is equally crucial for educators to motivate specialists involved in different activities crucial to the Third World—the agronomists, agriculturists, public health officials, cooperative administrators, veterinarians—to analyze the peasants' discourse, particularly in seminars where, we repeat, they would express how they see themselves in their associations with the world.

It's important that technicians overcome the distorted vision of their specialty, which transforms specialization into specialism, brutally forcing them into a narrow view of problems.

Agronomists, agriculturists, public health officials, cooperative administrators, literacy educators—we all have a lot to learn from peasants, and if we refuse to do so, we can't teach them anything.

Attempting to understand peasants' discourse will be a decisive step in overcoming that narrow view of problems typical of the specialist.

It is also possible to take advantage of these decodification tapes by discussing them with the same peasants and motivating them to dramatize the conditions under which they have lived and which they narrated in their discussions.

The word *struggle*, for instance, aroused lively discussion among various groups at different *asentamientos*. Peasants talked about what acquiring a deeper knowledge meant for them, specifically, the struggle to obtain the right to the land. In these discussions they related a little of their history not found in conventional textbooks. To dramatize these facts not only stimulates peasants' self-expression but also develops their political consciousness.

We can imagine the political-pedagogical reach this peasant discourse will have when these tapes begin to cover all areas of agrarian reform in Third World countries. This interchange could also be stimulated through a radio program run by the relevant government agency. This type of program might begin by broadcasting some of the taped debates, followed by commentaries in simple language by several educators.

There is something else that analysis of this discourse can provide: awareness of a series of issues relevant to the peasant communities that together constitute a theme that can be treated interdisciplinarily and can serve as a base for planning the educational content of postliteracy programs.

In thinking about what comes after literacy, why does one always think about a primary school program as an appropriate follow-up? It's as if adult literacy, whether fast paced or slow, were a necessary "treatment" to be administered, so that afterward one can go through the conventional primary school monotony. For this very reason, an adult literacy that breaks the traditional pattern must not extend into a postliteracy phase that negates the earlier progress.

The means of production must be linked to literacy, as is postliteracy to the *asentamiento;* so that literacy becomes an act, not just a transference, of knowledge. Using their concrete reality as a point of departure, peasants should find in their educational content the possibility of acquiring a knowledge of things and facts at an increasingly sophisticated level, and of seeing the reasons behind these facts.

Accordingly, supported by their experience, peasants should find in their postliteracy study in the *asentamiento* a more scientific understanding of their work and their reality.

Analysis of the taped decodifications sheds light on the basic areas of concern that can be expanded into learning units in various fields: agriculture, health, mathematics, ecology, geography, history, economics, and so on. The important thing is that each of these studies always be conducted in keeping with the concrete reality and experience of the peasants.

Finally, when the tape-recorded decodifications are transcribed, educators and peasant leaders should organize books and texts as peasant anthologies. These could be expanded by the inclusion of other texts written by educators and specialists, as we suggested in the first part of the chapter.

As with the tape recordings, these books should be shared with groups from other areas.

In studying their own text or the text of their peers from other areas, peasants would be studying discourse that evolved from the decodification of a theme.

After discussing, not merely reading, the previous discourse, they would criticize this discourse and create a new one, also to be tape-recorded. The discourse about the previous discourse, which involves knowledge of previous knowledge, would give rise to a new text, a second reading book proportionately richer, more critical, more pluralistic in its theme.

In this manner, one would be seriously attempting to develop the peasants' self-expression so that it can be critically introduced into the real world of the peasants' environment. This is a critical process through which peasants would more quickly gain a clear understanding that a particular system or way of living is the equivalent of a particular form of thought-language.

NOTES

1. For a definition of the term *generative word*, see chap.6, n.2.

2. For a definition of the term *codification*, see chap.6, n.14.

3. For a definition of the term *decodification*, see chap.6 n.15.

CHAPTER FOUR

Cultural Action and Agrarian Reform

G rounded in the system of the latifundium now in the process of being transformed into another transitional system, that of the *asentamiento* settlements, agrarian reform demands permanent critical thinking focused on this very act of transformation and its consequences.[1]

An ingenuous attitude toward this process, from which equally ingenuous tasks are derived, can lead to error and even fatal mistakes.

One mistake, for example, would be to reduce this transformation to a mechanical act by which the system of the latifundium merely yields to a new system of the *asentamiento*, as when someone mechanically substitutes one chair for another or moves a chair from one place to another.

The fundamental error that might appear even in the best of the acritical hypotheses is an attempt to deal with agrarian reform (which occurs in a historical-cultural, specifically human domain) in the same way one deals with things.

Mechanicism, technicism, and economicism are dimensions of the same acritical view of the agrarian reform process. All involve reducing peasants to pure objects of the transformation. With such a reformist overview, it is important to prescribe changes for and about peasants as if they were objects—rather than with peasants as fellow subjects of the transformation.

If it is necessary for peasants to adopt new technical procedures to increase production, then there is no alternative to extending to them specialist techniques that attempt to supplant their practical experience.

One forgets, however, that techniques, scientific knowledge, and the peasants' practical experience are culturally conditioned. In this sense, specialist techniques are as much cultural manifestations as are the practical experiences of the peasants.

Underestimating peasants' creativity and regenerative capacity, disregarding their knowledge at whatever level, trying to "fill" them with what technicians believe is right—all these are expressions of a dominant ideology. Yet having said this, we don't want to imply that peasants should stay where they are in terms of their confrontation with the natural world and national politics. We want to stress that they shouldn't be viewed as empty "vessels" into which one deposits knowledge. Quite the contrary, they too are subjects of a process of their beliefs.

A basic belief in an obviously necessary production increase doesn't need to be discussed. But what can and should be discussed is the manner of understanding and achieving this production increase.

In its focalist perception of the economic reality, the ingenuous viewpoint ignores the plain fact that there can be no production outside the relation man-world. The shortcoming of this viewpoint winds up transforming peasants into mere tools of production. Moreover, to the extent that one ignores that there is no production outside the relation man-world, one cannot grasp its importance.

Thus, one cannot or does not perceive that by transforming their work, men create their world. A world of culture and history, created by them, turns against them, conditioning them. This explains how culture becomes a product that is simultaneously capable of conditioning its creator.

It's obvious to us that an essential increase in agricultural production cannot be seen as something separate from the cultural universe where the increase takes place.

Obstacles to a production increase that technicians confront in the agrarian reform process are, by and large, of a cultural character. Peasants' resistance to more efficient, more productive work methods is, quite naturally, cultural.

Peasants develop their own way of seeing and understanding the world, according to cultural patterns that are obviously marked by the ideology of dominant groups in their global society. Their ways of thinking, conditioned by their behavior, which in turn conditions their thinking, have been developing and crystallizing over a long period of time. And if many of these old ways of thinking and behaving continue today, even where peasants find themselves struggling to defend their rights, it's even more reasonable to assume that these patterns continue among peasants who haven't had the same experience, in areas, for example, where agrarian reform came about without a struggle.

This explains why many cultural aspects of the latifundium continue in the transitional system of the *asentamiento*. Only a mechanicist would have trouble seeing that the superstructure cannot be automatically transformed by making changes in the infrastructure.

Further, the transformation of a society will be much more radical when it becomes an infrastructural process that renders the system a dialectic between the infrastructure and the superstructure. Many negative attributes of what we usually call the culture of silence, typical of closed systems like the latifundium, visibly force their way into the new system of the *asentamiento*.

This culture of silence, generated by the objective conditions of an oppressive reality, not only conditions behavior patterns of peasants while they are living in the infrastructure that produces oppression but also continues to condition behavior well after the infrastructure has been modified.

If the relationship that once existed between the dominant structure and the peasants' ways of viewing and behaving in the real world seems to be disappearing, this does not mean that in turn the negative effect of the culture of silence loses its conditioning force after the *asentamiento* is established. Its inhibiting power remains, not simply as an unimportant memory, but as a concrete interference with tasks the new system requires of the peasants. To thwart this inhibiting power, the peasants must be able to create new human relationships and a new style of life radically opposed to the previous one. These relationships must be characteristic of the newly established system and based on a different material reality. Even then, the culture of silence can occasionally "reactivate" itself under certain conditions, reappearing in its typical manifestations.

Only through the "dialect of superdeterminism" can we appreciate the persistent character of this "silence," which creates real problems even for revolutionary transformations.[2]

When we are equipped with methdological means, we can understand and explain peasants' fatalistic reaction to the challenges they face in their new reality. We also should understand that they frequently look to the dominating latifundium master as a model they must follow. Even when they're part of the *asentamiento*, it seems normal for them to allude to the old master in various ways, for example, in the expression "the true master lives above." In this expression of choosing this master as the real one, they are questioning the very validity of their state of *asentamiento*, a state in which they must overcome their previous role as objects and assume the new role of subjects. Then again, many find a new boss in the organization or agency that officially administers the agrarian reform.

These reactions cannot be understood by mechanicists. Ingenuously convinced of the automatic transformation of the superstructure by a change in the infrastructure, they tend antiscientifically to explain these reactions by characterizing peasants as "incapable and lazy," and sometimes as "ingrates" as well.

Instead of stimulating the peasants' decision-making power the mechanicists tend to act in a paternalistic manner, thereby reactivating the culture of silence and keeping peasants in a state of dependence. Mechanicists do nothing to help peasants overcome their fatalistic view of limiting situations; they do nothing to help peasants exchange their fatalism for another, critical vision, one capable of looking beyond these circumstances, one we call viable and unwritten.

Facing circumstances fatalistically, peasants search for reasons beyond the facts; they almost always find the answer in destiny or divine punishment.

At this point, a structural view of the problem resulting from the peasants' critical involvement is not really possible. Such a view is only possible when peasants actively participate in a political experience through a permanent mobilization. Defending their interests and recognizing that they cannot be antagonistic toward their peers (the urban workers), peasants are able to overcome the state that Goldman calls "real consciousness" through "maximal possible consciousness."[3]

To immobilize peasants by promoting a welfare syndrome is not a viable approach to overcoming their difficulties. Through this approach, peasants at best would be incorportated as objects into the agrarian reform process, but never incorporated within themselves in their role as subjects, never incorporated in agrarian reform as real subjects. Quite the contrary, by habit they would regularly confront the culture of silence and the projection of their myths would take over.

As long as this habit continues, the reality that mediates peasants as subjects abandons itself to a kind of self-admiration that remakes the peasants into objects in the relationship educators-learners and learners-educators. All of this necessitates that the *asentamiento*, while recognized as a unity of production, be understood also as a cultural unity. Then a peasant's introduction to a new technology would never be reduced to the transference of a list of techniques; it would be a truly creative activity. Once sure of their new technology, peasants should discuss the way they used to be "silenced" within the oppressive system of the latifundium.

Whereas the welfare syndrome of vertical and manipulative action necessarily involves a "cultural invasion," the kind of action we defend proposes a "cultural synthesis."[4] For this type of action to occur, action must be dialectical from the beginning.

Agronomists, agriculturists, literacy educators, cooperative administrators, and public health officials should meet with peasants dialectically, letting the very real world of the *asentamiento* function as mediator.

The role of an agent of action, adopted by those who have taken the initiative, ceases to belong solely to them when peasants also assume this role.

Cultural action oriented toward this synthesis begins with thematic investigation or generative themes through which peasants can begin a critical self-reflection and self-appraisal.

In presenting their own objective reality (how and where they are), as in problem solving, during a thematic investigation, peasants begin to revise their previous views of their real world through codified situations. They will then achieve an understanding of their previous knowledge.[5] In so doing, they expand the limits of knowledge, appreciating in their "deep vision" the dimensions that up to then were not understood and are now perceived by them as "clearly understood."

Again, this type of cultural action can only make sense when one tries to present it as a theoretical instance of social experience in which peasants participate. If one is alienated from this experience, one loses oneself, emptied in a series of nonsense syllables.

Finally, cultural action, as we understand it, cannot be superimposed on the peasants' world vision; it cannot invade them and require that they adapt themselves to it. On the contrary, in establishing this vision as a starting point and seeing it as a kind of problem to be solved, the educator exercises with the peasants a critical evaluation of their world view, resulting in their increasingly clearer involvement with the real world in transformation.

NOTES

1. For a definition, see preface.

2. Louis Althusser, *Pour Marx*, François Maspéro, Paris, 1967.

3. Lucien Goldman, *Las Ciencias humanas y la filosofia*, Edición Nueva Visión, Buenos Aires.

4. For more details on "Cultural invasion" and "Cultural synthesis", see Paulo Freire, *Pedagogy of the Oppressed*.

5. See Paulo Freire, *Pedagogy of the Oppressed*.

CHAPTER FIVE

The Social Worker's Role in the Process of Change

To understand "the social worker's role in the process of change," we should begin by reflecting on these very words that articulate our theme. These words show us the sum of their meaning. Our inward critical analysis will let us see the interaction of these terms as a genesis of structured thinking that incorporates a significant message.

In leading us to a deeper meaning, our inward and critical analysis ought to surpass any notion of a simplistic overview that repeatedly leaves us on the surface of whatever we discuss.

In the critical view we are here defending, the act of looking implies another, that of "admiring."[1] We admire and in our looking deeply into what we admire, we look inward and from within; this makes us see.

In the naive view (our "unarmed" way of confronting reality), we merely look but we can't see because we don't admire what we look at in its intimacy (that which leads us to see what was purely looked at).

It is important, then, that we admire the words of our proposed theme so that in looking at them from the inside we can recognize that they ought not to be dealt with as a mere cliché. This theme is not a slogan; it's a problem in itself and a challenge.

While just looking at these words and so remaining in their periphery, we might limit ourselves to talking about their message as one of "ready-made ideas."

In critically and inwardly analyzing this message we have a chance to break down its constituent parts. Dividing the totality into its components enables us to return to the totality with a more in-depth comprehension of its meaning.

Admiring, looking inward, dividing the totality so we can return to look at what's admired (that is, to move toward the totality and return from it to its parts)—these can be separate acts only when the mind has to think abstractly to reach what's concrete. In reality, these are acts that mutually involve one another.

By admiring these words that involve a challenging theme and by breaking down their components, we find that the term *role* is modified by a restrictive expression (a noun in the possessive case) that delimits its "extension": *social worker*. Here, though, there is a qualifying term, *social*, that is closely tied to one's "comprehension" of the term *worker*.

This subunity of the general structure of one phrase, *the role of the social worker*, is linked to the second phrase, *in the process of change*, which according to the meaning in the message represents "where" *the role* is met, through the preposition *in*.

In truth, the role of the social worker does not take place in the process of change, as a purely grammatical reading suggests. The role of the social worker develops itself in a broader domain where change is one aspect. The social worker, along with others, acts in a social structure.

In this way we must grasp the full complexity of this message. Critically speaking, for anything to be, it has to be in the process of being. What characterizes the social structure is, in fact, neither change nor permanence, but the "duration" of the contradiction between both of these, given that one predominates over the other.

Although there is a dialectic between the infrastructure and the superstructure, there is no permanence of permanence, or change of change in the social structure; but the aim of preserving the social structure contradicts the effort to change it. Therefore, one cannot be a social worker and be like the educator who's a coldly neutral technician. To keep our options secret, to conceal them in the cobwebs of technique, or to disguise them by claiming neutrality does not constitute neutrality; quite the contrary, it helps maintain the status quo.

Accordingly, we need to clarify our political options through experience that is also political.

It's naive to consider our role as abstract in a matrix of neutral methods and techniques for action that doesn't take place in a neutral reality.

If a social worker chooses reactionary options, his or her methodology and work will be oriented toward blocking change. Rather than perceiving the social worker's task as one by which, through a critical, common effort, reality unveils itself to him and to those with whom he works, he'll be preoccupied with mythicizing reality. Instead of developing opportunities for problem–posing to challenge her and the men and women with whom she should be communicating, her tendency will be to favor welfare–syndrome solutions. In short, through his or her actions and reactions, this type of social worker is motivated to assist in the "normalization" of the "established order," which serves the power elite's interests.

The social worker who chooses this option can (and almost always tries to) disguise it, appearing to be for change and thus keeping to a quasi transformation, which is one way not to change.

One of the signals that social workers have chosen reactionary options is their discomfort over the consequences of change, their distrust of the new, and (sometimes impossible to hide) their fears of losing "social status." There is no room in their methodologies for communication, critical reflection, creativity, or collaboration; there is only room for ostensible manipulation.

Indeed, a reactionary social worker can't be interested in individuals' developing a critical view of their reality, that is, in their thinking about what they do while they actually do it. This returning to perception on perception, conditioned by reality, doesn't interest a reactionary.

Through their own thought and actions, people can see the conditioning of perception in their social structure, and in this way their perception begins to change, even though this does not yet mean a change in the social structure. It's important to appreciate that social reality can be transformed; that it is made by men and can be changed by men; that it is not something untouchable, a fate or destiny that offers only one choice: accommodation. It's essential that the naive view of reality give way to a view that is capable of perceiving itself, that fatalism be supplanted by a critical optimism that can move individuals toward an increasingly critical commitment for radical change in society. A reactionary social worker is not interested in any of this.

Some say that a change of perception is not possible before a change in the social structure because perception is conditioned by society. But this kind of thinking, from an extremist point of view, can lead us to mechanistic interpretations of the relations between perception and reality.

On the other hand, to avoid confusion between our position and an idealist attitude, we should say something more about this process.

A change in the perception of reality can take place before the transformation of reality if one doesn't attach to the term *before* a sense of a stagnated time dimension from which one can infer only ingenuous consciousness.

The meaning of *before* here is not the usual meaning. The word *before* does not mean a previous moment, separated from another by a rigid boundary. *Before* is part of the structural transformation process.

Perception of reality, then, through the perspective of the dominant ideology, can be changed to the extent that when one verifies "today" the antagonism between change and permanence, this antagonism begins to be a challenge.

This change of perception, which occurs in the "problematizing" of a reality in conflict, in viewing our problems in life in their true context, requires us to reconfront our reality. Not "sticking" to it, we need to "appropriate" the context and insert ourselves in it, not *under* time, but already *in* time.

If this kind of effort can't be developed by the reactionary social worker, it ought to be a constant preoccupation for those committed to change. Their roles and methodologies, of course, will be quite different from those of reactionaries.

First, by claiming that neutrality of action cannot exist and by refusing to administer to individuals or groups or communities through purely anaesthetic forms of action, the social worker who opts for change strives to unveil reality. She or he works *with*, never *on*, people whom she or he considers subjects, not objects or incidences, of action. As one who is humble and critical, she or he cannot accept the ingenuity embodied in the "ready-made idea" generalized in such a way that the social worker appears as the "agent of change." This act of refusal is not just for some of us but for all who are committed to change.

The social worker who opts for change does not fear freedom, nor will this person prescribe or manipulate; but in rejecting prescription and manipulation, this person rejects thoughtless spontaneity as well.

She or he knows that all attempts at making a radical transformation of society require a conscious organization of the oppressed and that this calls for a lucid vanguard. If this vanguard cannot be the "proprietor" over others, by the same token it cannot be totally passive.

Moreover, it would be illusory to think that with this line of reasoning a social worker could move freely, as though dominant groups weren't alert to the need for defending their own interests. Along with the idea that certain changes of an obviously reformist character are needed, there are some real cautions.

It's most important for social workers to recognize the reality they confront and its "viable history" as well. In other words, we should recognize what can be done in any given moment, since we do what we can and not what we would like to do.

This means we need to have a clear understanding of the relationships between tactics and strategy, which are, unfortunately, not always seriously considered.

NOTES

1. For a discussion of "admiring," see chap. 6.

CHAPTER SIX

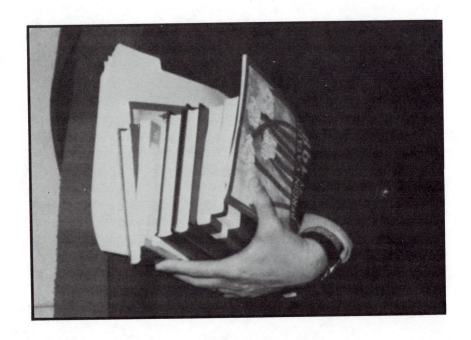

The Adult Literacy Process as Cultural Action for Freedom*

Every Educational Practice Implies a Concept of Man and the World

Experience teaches us not to assume that the obvious is clearly understood.[1] So it is with the truism with which we begin: All educational practice implies a theoretical stance on the educator's part. This stance in turn implies—sometimes more, sometimes less explicitly—an interpretation of man and the world. It could not be otherwise. The process of men's orientation in the world involves not just the association of sense images, as for animals. It involves, above all, thought-language,

*This chapter was translated by Loretta Slover

43

that is, the possibility of the act of knowing through his praxis, by which man transforms reality. For man, this process of orientation in the world can be understood neither as a purely subjective event, nor as an objective or mechanistic one, but only as an event in which subjectivity and objectivity are united. Orientation in the world, so understood, places the question of the purposes of action at the level of critical perception of reality.

If, for animals, orientation in the world means adaptation to the world, for man it means humanizing the world by transforming it. For animals there is no historical sense, no options or values in their orientation in the world; for man there is both an historical and a value dimension. Men have the sense of "project," in contrast to the instinctive routines of animals.

The action of men without objectives, whether the objectives are right or wrong, mythical or demythologized, naive or critical, is not praxis, though it may be orientation in the world. And not being praxis, it is action ignorant both of its own process and of its aim. The interrelation of the awareness of aim and of process is the basis for planning action, which implies methods, objectives, and value options.

Teaching adults to read and write must be seen, analyzed, and understood in this way. The critical analyst will discover, in the methods and texts used by educators and students, practical value options that betray a philosophy of man, well or poorly outlined, coherent or incoherent. Only someone with a mechanistic mentality, which Marx would call grossly materialistic, could reduce adult literacy learning to a purely technical action. Such a naive approach would be incapable of perceiving that technique itself as an instrument of men in their orientation in the world is not neutral. We shall try, however, to prove by analysis the self-evidence of our statement.

The Illiterate as the Empty Man

Let us consider the case of primers used as the basic texts for teaching adults to read and write. Let us further propose two distinct types: a poorly done primer and a good one, according to the genre's own criteria. Let us even suppose that the author of the good primer based the selection of its generative words on a prior knowledge of which words have the greatest resonance for the learner (a practice not commonly found, though it does exist).[2]

Doubtlessly, such an author is already far beyond the colleague who composes his primer with words he himself chooses in his own library. Both authors, however, are identical in a fundamental way. In each case they themselves decompose the given generative words and from the syllables create new words. With these words, in turn, the authors form simple sentences and, little by little, small stories, the so-called reading lessons.

Let us say that the author of the second primer, going one step further, suggests that the teachers who use it initiate discussions about one or another word, sentence, or text with their students.

After considering either of these hypothetical cases, we may legitimately conclude that there is an implicit concept of man in the primer's method and content, whether it is recognized by the authors or not. This concept can be reconstructed from various angles. We begin with the fact, inherent in the idea and use of the primer, that it is the teacher who chooses the words and proposes them to the learner. Insofar as the primer is the mediating object between the teacher and students, and the students are to be "filled" with words the teachers have chosen, one can easily detect a first important dimension of the image of man that here begins to emerge. It is the profile of a man whose consciousness is "spatialized," and must be "filled" or "fed" in order to know. This same conception led Sartre, criticizing the notion that "to know is to eat," to exclaim, *"O philosophie alimentaire!"*[3]

This "nutritionist" concept of knowledge, so common in current educational practice, is found very clearly in the primer.[4] Illiterates are considered "undernourished," not in the literal sense in which many of them really are, but because they lack the "bread of the spirit." Consistent with the concept of knowledge as food, illiteracy is conceived of as a "poison herb," intoxicating and debilitating persons who cannot read or write. Thus, much is said about the "eradication" of illiteracy to cure the disease.[5] In this way, deprived of their character as linguistic signs constitutive of man's thought-language, words are transformed into mere "deposits of vocabulary"—the bread of the spirit that the illiterates are to "eat" and "digest."

This "nutritionist" view of knowledge perhaps also explains the humanitarian character of certain Third World adult literacy campaigns. If millions of men are illiterate, "starving for letters," "thirsty for words," the word must be *brought* to them to save them from "hunger" and "thirst." The word, according to the naturalistic concept of consciousness implicit in the primer, must be "deposited," not born of the creative effort of the learners. As understood in this concept, man is a passive being, the object of the process of learning to read and write, and not its subject. As an object his task is to "study" the so-called reading lessons, which in fact are almost completely alienating and alienated, having so little, if anything, to do with the student's sociocultural reality.[6]

It would be a truly interesting study to analyze the reading texts being used in private or official adult literacy campaigns in rural and urban areas of Third World countries. It would not be unusual to find among such texts sentences and readings like the following random samples:[7]

A asa é da ave—"The wing is of the bird."
Eva viu a uva—"Eva saw the grape."
O galo canta—"The cock crows."
O cachorro ladra—"The dog barks."
Maria gosta dos animais—"Mary likes animals."
João cuida das árvores—"John takes care of the trees."
  O pai de Carlinhos se chama António. Carlinhos é um bom menino, bem comportado e estudioso—"Charles's father's name is Antonio. Charles is a good, well-behaved, and studious boy."
  Ada deu o dedo ao urubu? Duvido, Ada deu o dedo a arara. . . .[8]
  Se você trabalha com martelo e prego, tenha cuidado para não furar o dedo—"If you hammer a nail, be careful not to smash your finger."

Peter did not know how to read. Peter was ashamed. One day, Peter went to school and registered for a night course. Peter's teacher was very good. Peter knows how to read now. Look at Peter's face. [These lessons are generally illustrated.] Peter is smiling. He is a happy man. He already has a good job. Everyone ought to follow his example.

In saying that Peter is smiling because he knows how to read, that he is happy because he now has a good job, and that he is an example for all to follow, the authors establish a relationship between knowing how to read and getting good jobs that, in fact, cannot be borne out. This naiveté reveals, at least, a failure to perceive the structure not only of illiteracy but of social phenomena in general. Such an approach may admit that these phenomena exist, but it cannot perceive their relationship to the structure of the society in which they are found. It is as if these phenomena were mythical, above and beyond concrete situations, or the results of the intrinsic inferiority of a certain class of men. Unable to grasp contemporary illiteracy as a typical manifestation of the "culture of silence," directly related to underdeveloped structures, this approach cannot offer an objective, critical response to the challenge of illiteracy. Merely teaching men to read and write does not work miracles; if there are not enough jobs for men able to work, teaching more men to read and write will not create them.

One of these readers presents among its lessons the following two texts on consecutive pages without relating them. The first is about May 1, the Labor Day holiday, on which workers commemorate their struggles. It does not say how or where these are commemorated, or what the nature of the historical conflict was. The main theme of the second lesson is holidays. It says that "on these days people ought to go to the beach to swim and sunbathe. . . ." Therefore, if May 1 is a holiday, and if on holidays people should go to the beach, the conclusion is that the workers should go swimming on Labor Day, instead of meeting with their unions in the public squares to discuss their problems.

Analysis of these texts reveals, then, a simplistic vision of men, of their world, of the relationship between the two, and of the literacy process that unfolds in that world.

A asa é da ave, Eva viu a uva, O galo canta, and *O cachorro ladra* are linguistic contexts that, when mechanically memorized and repeated, are deprived of their authentic dimension as thought-language in dynamic interplay with reality. Thus impoverished, they are not authentic expressions of the world.

Their authors do not recognize in the poor classes the ability to know and even create the texts that would express their own thought-language at the level of their perception of the world. The authors repeat with the texts what they do with the words, that is, they introduce them into the learners' consciousness as if it were empty space—once more, the nutritionist concept of knowledge.

The Illiterate as the Marginal Man

Still more, the astructural perception of illiteracy revealed in these texts exposes the other false view of illiterates as marginal men.[9] Those who consider them marginal must, nevertheless, recognize the existence of a reality to which they are marginal—not only physical space, but historical, social, cultural, and economic realities—that is, the structural dimension of reality. In this way, illiterates have to be recognized as beings "outside of," "marginal to" something, since it is impossible to be marginal to nothing. But being "outside of" or "marginal to" necessarily implies a movement of the one said to be marginal from the center, where he was, to the periphery. This movement, which is an action, presupposes in turn not only an agent but also his reasons. Admitting the existence of men "outside of" or "marginal to" structural reality, we may legitimately ask: who is the author of this movement from the center of the structure to its margin? Do so-called marginal men, among them the illiterates, make the decision to move out to the periphery of society? If so, marginality is an option with all that it involves: hunger, sickness, rickets, pain, mental deficiencies, living death, crime, promiscuity, despair, the impossibility of being. In fact, however, it is difficult to accept that 40 percent of Brazil's population, almost 90 percent of Haiti's, 60 percent of Bolivia's, about 40 percent of Peru's, more than 30 percent of Mexico's and Venezuela's, and about 70 percent of Guatemala's would have made the tragic *choice* of their own marginality as illiterates.[10] If, then, marginality is not by choice, marginal man has been expelled from and kept outside of the social system and is therefore the object of violence.

In fact, however, the social structure as a whole does not "expel," nor is marginal man a "being outside of." He is, on the contrary, a "being inside of," within the social structure, and in a dependent relationship to those whom we call falsely autonomous beings, inauthentic "beings for themselves."

A less rigorous approach, one more simplistic, less critical, more technicist, would say that it was unnecessary to reflect on what it would consider unimportant questions such as illiteracy and teaching adults to read and write. Such an approach might even add that the discussion of the concept of marginality is an unnecessary academic exercise. In fact, however, it is not so. In accepting the illiterate as a person who exists on the fringe of society, we are led to envision him as a sort of "sick man," for whom literacy would be the "medicine" to cure him, enabling him to "return" to the "healthy" structure from which "he has become separated." Educators would be benevolent counselors, scouring the outskirts of the city for the stubborn illiterates, runaways from the good life, to restore them to the forsaken bosom of happiness by giving them the gift of the word.

In the light of such a concept—unfortunately, all too widespread—literacy programs can never be efforts toward freedom; they will never question the very reality that deprives men of the right to speak up—not only illiterates but all those who are treated as objects in a dependent relationship. These men, illiterate or not, are in fact not marginal. What we said before bears repeating: They are not "beings outside of"; they are "beings for another." Therefore the solution to their problem is to become, not "beings inside of," but men freeing themselves; for, in reality, they are not marginal to the structure, but oppressed men within it. Alienated men, they cannot overcome their dependency by "incorporation" into the very structure responsible for their dependency. There is no other road to humanization—theirs as well as everyone else's—other than authentic transformation of the dehumanizing structure.

From this last point of view, the illiterate is no longer a person living on the fringe of society, a marginal man, but rather a representative of the dominated strata of society, in conscious or unconscious opposition to those who, in the same structure, treat him as a thing. Thus, also, teaching men to read and write is no longer an inconsequential matter of *ba, be, bi, bo, bu,* of memorizing an alienated word, but a difficult apprenticeship in naming the world.

In the first hypothesis, interpreting illiterates as men marginal to society, the literacy process reinforces the mythicization of reality by keeping it opaque and by dulling the "empty consciousness" of the learner with innumerable alienating words and phrases. By contrast, in the second hypothesis, viewing illiterates as men oppressed within the system, the literacy process, as cultural action for freedom, is an act of knowing in which the learner assumes the role of knowing subject in dialogue with the educator. For this very reason, it is a courageous endeavor to demythologize reality, a process through which men who had previously been submerged in reality begin to emerge in order to reinsert themselves into it with critical awareness.

Therefore the educator must strive for an ever greater clarity of what, at times without his conscious knowledge, illumines the path of his action. Only in this way will he truly be able to assume the role of one of the subjects of this action and remain consistent in the process.

The Adult Literacy Process as an Act of Knowing

To be an act of knowing, the adult literacy process demands among teachers and students a relationship of authentic dialogue. True dialogue unites subjects together in the cognition of a knowable object, which mediates between them.

If learning to read and write is to constitute an act of knowing, the learners must assume from the beginning the role of creative subjects.

It is not a matter of memorizing and repeating given syllables, words, and phrases, but rather of reflecting critically on the process of reading and writing itself, and on the profound significance of language.

Insofar as language is impossible without thought, and language and thought are impossible without the world to which they refer, the human word is more than mere vocabulary—it is word-and-action. The cognitive dimensions of the literacy process must include the relationships of men with their world. These relationships are the source of the dialectic between the products men achieve in transforming the world and the conditioning these products in turn exercise on men.

Learning to read and write ought to be an opportunity for men to know what *speaking the word* really means: a human act implying reflection and action. As such it is a primordial human right and not the privilege of a few.[11] Speaking the word is not a true act if it is not at the same time associated with the right of self-expression and world-expression, of creating and re-creating, of deciding and choosing and ultimately participating in society's historical process.

In the culture of silence the masses are mute, that is, they are prohibited from creatively taking part in the transformations of their society and therefore prohibited from being. Even if they can occasionally read and write because they were "taught" in humanitarian—but not humanist—literacy campaigns, they are nevertheless alienated from the power responsible for their silence.

Illiterates know they are concrete men. They know that they do things. What they do not know in the culture of silence—in which they are ambiguous, dual beings—is that men's actions as such are transforming, creative, and re-creative. Overcome by the myths of this culture, including the myth of their own "natural inferiority," they do not know that *their* action upon the world is also transforming. Prevented from having a "structural perception" of the facts involving them, they do not know that they cannot "have a voice," that is, that they cannot exercise the right to participate consciously in the sociohistorical transformation of their society, because their work does not belong to them.

It could be said (and we would agree) that it is not possible to recognize all this apart from praxis, that is, apart from reflection and action, and that to attempt it would be pure idealism. But it is also true that action upon an object must be critically analyzed in order to understand both the object itself and the understanding one has of it. The act of knowing involves a dialectical movement that goes from action to reflection and from reflection upon action to a new action. For the learner to know what he did not know before, he must engage in an authentic process of abstraction by means of which he can reflect on the action-object whole, or, more generally, on forms of orientation in the world. In this process of abstraction, situations representative of how the learner orients himself in the world are proposed to him as the objects of his critique.

As an event calling forth the critical reflection of both the learners and educators, the literacy process must relate *speaking the word* to *transforming reality*, and to man's role in this transformation. Perceiving the significance of that relationship is indispensable for those learning to read and write if we are really committed to liberation. Such a perception will lead the learners to recognize a much greater right than that of being literate. They will ultimately recognize that, as men, they have the right to have a voice.

On the other hand, as an act of knowing, learning to read and write presupposes not only a theory of knowing but a method that corresponds to the theory.

We recognize the indisputable unity between subjectivity and objectivity in the act of knowing. Reality is never just simply the objective datum, the concrete fact, but is also men's perception of it. Once again, this is not a subjectivistic or idealistic affirmation, as it might seem. On the contrary, subjectivism and idealism come into play when the subjective-objective unity is broken.[12]

The adult literacy process as an act of knowing implies the existence of two interrelated contexts. One is the context of authentic dialogue between learners and educators as equally knowing subjects. This is what schools should be—the theoretical context of dialogue. The second is the real, concrete context of facts, the social reality in which men exist.[13]

In the theoretical context of dialogue, the facts presented by the real or concrete context are critically analyzed. This analysis involves the exercise of abstraction, through which, by means of representations of concrete reality, we seek knowledge of that reality. The instrument for this abstraction in our methodology is codification, or representation of the existential situations of the learners.[14]

Codification, on the one hand, mediates between the concrete and theoretical contexts (of reality). On the other hand, as knowable object, it mediates between the knowing subjects, educators and learners, who seek in dialogue to unveil the action-object wholes.

This type of linguistic discourse must be "read" by anyone who tries to interpret it, even when purely pictorial. As such, it presents what Chomsky calls surface structure and deep structure.

The surface structure of codification makes the action-object whole explicit in a purely taxonomic form. The first stage of decodification—or reading—is descriptive.[15] At this stage, the "readers"—or decodifiers—focus on the relationship between the categories constituting the codification. This preliminary focus on the surface structure is followed by "problematizing" the codified situation. This leads the learner to the second and fundamental stage of decodification, the comprehension of the codification's deep structure. By understanding the codification's deep structure the learner can then understand the dialectic that exists between the categories presented in the surface structure, as well as the unity between the surface and deep structures.

In our method, the codification initially takes the form of a photograph or sketch that represents a real existent, or an existent constructed by the learners. When this representation is projected as a slide, the learners effect an operation basic to the fact of knowing: they gain distance from the knowable object. This experience of distance is undergone as well by the educators, so that educators and learners together can reflect critically on the knowable object that mediates between them. The aim of decodification is to arrive at the critical level of knowing, beginning with the learner's experience of the situation in the "real context."

Whereas the codified representation is the knowable object mediating between knowing subjects, decodification—dissolving the codification into its constituent elements—is the operation by which the knowing subjects perceive relationships between the codification's elements and other facts presented by the real context, relationships that were formerly unperceived. Codification represents a given dimension of reality as individuals live it, and this dimension is proposed for their analysis in a context other than that in which they live it. Codification thus transforms what was a way of life in the real context into "objectum" in the theoretical context. The learners, rather than receive information about this or that fact, analyze aspects of their own existential experience represented in the codification.

Existential experience is a whole. In illuminating one of its facets and perceiving the interrelation of that facet with others, the learners tend to replace a fragmented vision of reality with a total vision. From the point of view of a theory of knowledge, this means that the dynamic between codification of existential situations and decodification involves the learners in a constant reconstruction of their former "admiration" of reality.

We do not use the concept of admiration here in the usual way, or in its ethical or aesthetic sense, but with a special philosophical connotation.

To admire is to objectify the "not I." It is a dialectical operation that characterizes man as man, differentiating him from the animal. It is directly associated with the creative dimension of his language. *To admire* implies that man stands over against his "not I" in order to understand it. For this reason, there is no act of knowing without admiration of the object to be known. If the act of knowing is a dynamic act—and no knowledge is ever complete—then in order to know, man not only admires the object, but must always be readmiring his former admiration. When we readmire our former admiration (always an admiration *of*), we are simultaneously admiring the act of admiring and the object admired, so that we can overcome the errors we made in our former admiration. This readmiration leads us to a perception of an anterior perception.

In the process of decodifying representations of their existential situations and perceiving former perceptions, the learners gradually, hesitatingly, and timorously place in doubt the opinion they held of reality and replace it with a more and more critical knowledge.

Let us suppose that we were to present to groups from among the dominated classes codifications that portray their imitation of the dominators' cultural models—a natural tendency of the oppressed consciousness at a given moment.[16] The dominated persons would perhaps, in self-defense, deny the truth of the codification. As they deepened their analysis, however, they would begin to perceive that their apparent imitation of the dominators' models is a result of their interiorization of these models and, above all, of the myths of the superiority of the dominant classes that cause the dominated to feel inferior. What in fact is pure interiorization appears in a naive analysis to be imitation. At bottom, when the dominated classes reproduce the dominators' style of life, it is because the dominators live "within" the dominated. The dominated can eject the dominators only by getting distance from them and objectifying them. Only then can they recognize them as their antithesis.[17]

To the extent, however, that interiorization of the dominators' values is not only an individual phenomenon but also a social and cultural one, ejection must be achieved by a type of cultural action in which culture negates culture. That is, culture, as an interiorized product that in turn conditions men's subsequent acts, must become the object of men's knowledge so that they can perceive its conditioning power. Cultural action occurs at the level of superstucture. It can only be understood by what Althusser calls the dialectic of overdetermination.[18] This analytic tool prevents us from falling into mechanistic explanations or, what is worse, mechanistic action. An understanding of it precludes surprise that cultural myths remain after the infrastructure is transformed, even by revolution.

When the creation of a new culture is appropriate but impeded by interiorized cultural "residue," this residue, these myths, must be expelled by means of culture. Cultural action and cultural revolution, at different stages, constitute the modes of this expulsion.

The learners must discover the reasons behind many of their attitudes toward cultural reality and thus confront cultural reality in a new way. Readmiration of their former admiration is necessary in order to bring this about. The learners' capacity for critical knowing—well beyond mere opinion—is established in the process of unveiling their relationships with the historical-cultural world *in* and *with* which they exist.

We do not mean to suggest that critical knowledge of man-world relationships arises as a verbal knowledge outside of praxis. Praxis is involved in the concrete situations that are codified for critical analysis. To analyze the codification in its deep structure is, for this very reason, to reconstruct the former praxis and to become capable of a new and different praxis. The relationship between the theoretical context, in which codified representations of objective facts are analyzed, and the concrete context, where these facts occur, has to be made real.

Such education must have the character of commitment. It implies a movement from the concrete context, which provides objective facts, to the theoretical context, where these facts are analyzed in depth, and back to the concrete context, where men experiment with new forms of praxis.

Dialogue as Methodology

It might seem as if some of our statements defend the principle that, whatever the level of the learners, they ought to reconstruct the process of human knowing in absolute terms. In fact, when we consider adult literacy learning or education in general as an act of knowing, we are advocating a synthesis between the educator's maximally systematized knowing and the learners' minimally systematized knowing—a synthesis achieved in dialogue. The educator's role is to propose problems about the codified existential situations in order to help the learners arrive at a more and more critical view of their reality. The educator's responsibility as conceived by this philosophy is thus greater in every way than that of his colleague whose duty is to transmit information that the learners memorize. Such an educator can simply repeat what he has read, and often misunderstood, since education for him does not mean an act of knowing.

The first type of educator, on the contrary, is a knowing subject, face to face with other knowing subjects. He can never be a mere memorizer, but a person constantly readjusting his knowledge who calls forth knowledge from his students. For him, education is a pedagogy of knowing. The educator whose approach is mere memorization is anti-dialogical; his act of transmitting knowledge is inalterable. For the educator who experiences the act of knowing together with his students, in contrast, dialogue is the sign of the act of knowing. He is aware, however, that not all dialogue is in itself the mark of a relationship of true knowledge.

Socratic intellectualism—which mistook the definition of the concept for knowledge of the thing defined and this knowledge as virtue— did not constitute a true pedagogy of knowing, even though it was dialogical. Plato's theory of dialogue failed to go beyond the Socratic theory of the definition as knowledge, even though for Plato one of the necessary conditions for knowing was that man be capable of a *prise de conscience*, and though the passage from *doxa* to *logos* was indispensable for man to achieve truth. For Plato, the *prise de conscience* did not refer to what man knew or did not know or knew badly about his dialectical relationship with the world; it was concerned rather with what man once knew and forgot at birth. To know was to remember or recollect forgotten knowledge. The apprehension of both *doxa* and *logos* and the overcoming of *doxa* by *logos* occurred, not in the man-world relationship, but in the effort to remember or rediscover a forgotten *logos*.

For dialogue to be a method of true knowledge, the knowing subjects must approach reality scientifically in order to seek the dialectical connections that explain the form of reality. Thus, to know is not to remember something previously known and now forgotten. Nor can *doxa* be overcome by *logos* apart from the dialectical relationship of man with his world, apart from men's reflective action upon the world.

To be an act of knowing, then, the adult literacy process must engage the learners in the constant problematizing of their existential situations. This problematizing employs generative words chosen by specialized educators in a preliminary investigation of what we call the minimal linguistic universe of the future learners. The words are chosen (a) for their pragmatic value, that is, as linguistic signs that command a common understanding in a region or area of the same city or country (in the United States, for instance, the word *soul* has a special significance in black areas that it does not have among whites), and (b) for their phonetic difficulties, which will gradually be presented to those learning to read and write. Finally, it is important that the first generative word be trisyllabic. When it is divided into its syllables, each one constituting a syllabic family, the learners can experiment with various syllabic combinations even at first sight of the word.

Having chosen seventeen generative words, the next step is to codify seventeen existential situations familiar to the learners. [19] The generative words are then worked into the situations one by one in the order of their increasing phonetic difficulty. As we have already emphasized, these codifications are knowable objects that mediate between the knowing subjects, educator-learners, learner-educators. Their act of knowing is elaborated in the *círculo de cultura* (cultural discussion group), which functions as the theoretical context.

In Brazil, before analyzing the learners' existential situations and the generative words contained in them, we proposed the codified theme of man-world relationships in general. [20] In Chile, at the suggestion of Chilean educators, this important dimension was discussed concurrently with learning to read and write. What is important is that the person learning words be concomitantly engaged in a critical analysis of the social framework in which men exist. For example, the word *favela* in Rio de Janeiro, Brazil, and the word *callampa* in Chile represent, each with its own nuances, the same social, economic, and cultural reality of the vast numbers of slum dwellers in those countries. If *favela* and *callampa* are used as generative words for the people of Brazilian and Chilean slums, respectively, the codification will have to represent slum situations.

There are many people who consider slum dwellers marginal, intrinsically wicked and inferior. To such people we recommend the profitable experience of discussing the slum situation with slum dwellers themselves. Since some of these critics are often simply mistaken, it is possible that they may rectify their mythical clichés and assume a more scientific attitude. They may avoid saying that the illiteracy, alcoholism, and crime of the slums, that its sickness, infant mortality, learning deficiencies, and poor hygiene, reveal the "inferior nature" of its inhabitants. They may even end up realizing that if intrinsic evil exists it is part of the structures, and that it is the structures that need to be transformed.

It should be pointed out that the Third World as a whole, and more in some parts than in others, suffers from the same misunderstanding among certain sectors of the so-called metropolitan societies. They see the Third World as the incarnation of evil, the primitive, the devil, sin and sloth—in sum, as historically unviable without the director societies. Such a Manichaean attitude is at the source of the impulse to "save" the "demon-possessed" Third World, "educating it" and "correcting its thinking" according to the director societies' own criteria.

The expansionist interests of the director societies are implicit in such notions. These societies can never relate to the Third World as partners, since partnership presupposes equals, no matter how different the equal parties may be, and can never be established between parties antagonistic to each other.

Thus, "salvation" of the Third World by the director societies can only mean its domination, whereas in its legitimate aspiration to independence lies its utopian vision: to save the director societies in the very act of freeing itself.

In this sense the pedagogy that we defend, conceived in a significant area of the Third World, is itself a utopian pedagogy. By this very fact it is full of hope, for to be utopian is not to be merely idealistic or impractical but rather to engage in denunciation and annunciation. Our pedagogy cannot do without a vision of man and of the world. It formulates a scientific humanist conception that finds its expression in a dialogical praxis in which the teachers and learners together, in the act of analyzing a dehumanizing reality, denounce it while announcing its transformation in the name of the liberation of man.

For this very reason, denunciation and annunciation in this utopian pedagogy are not meant to be empty words, but an historic commitment. Denunciation of a dehumanizing situation today increasingly demands precise scientific understanding of that situation. Similarly, the annunciation of its transformation increasingly requires a theory of transforming action. Yet, neither act by itself implies the transformation of the denounced reality or the establishment of that which is announced. Rather, as a moment in a historical process, the announced reality is already present in the act of denunciation and annunciation.[21]

That is why the utopian character of our educational theory and practice is as permanent as education itself, which for us is cultural action. Its thrust toward denunciation and annunciation cannot be exhausted when the reality denounced today cedes its place tomorrow to the reality previously announced in the denunciation. When education is no longer utopian, that is, when it no longer embodies the dramatic unity of denunciation and annunciation, it is either because the future has no more meaning for men, or because men are afraid to risk living the future as creative overcoming of the present, which has become old.

The more likely explanation is generally the latter. That is why some people today study all the possibilities the future contains, in order to "domesticate" it and keep it in line with the present, which is what they intend to maintain. If there is any anguish in director societies hidden beneath the cover of their cold technology, it springs from their desperate determination that their metropolitan status be preserved in the future. Among the things the Third World may learn from the metropolitan societies there is this that is fundamental: not to replicate those societies when its current utopia becomes fact.

When we defend such a conception of education—realistic precisely to the extent that it is utopian, that is, to the extent that it denounces what in fact is, and finds therefore between denunciation and its realization the time of its praxis—we are attempting to formulate a type of education that corresponds to the specifically human mode of being, which is historical.

There is no annunciation without denunciation, just as every denunciation generates annunciation. Without the latter, hope is impossible. In an authentic utopian vision, however, hoping does not mean folding one's arms and waiting. Waiting is only possible when one, filled with hope, seeks through reflective action to achieve that announced future which is being born within the denunciation.

That is why there is no genuine hope in those who intend to make the future repeat their present, or in those who see the future as something predetermined. Both have a domesticated notion of history: the former because they want to stop time, the latter because they are certain about a future they already "know." Utopian hope, on the contrary, is engagement full of risk. That is why the dominators, who merely denounce those who denounce them and have nothing to announce but the preservation of the status quo, can never be utopian or, for that matter, prophetic.[22]

A utopian pedagogy of denunciation and annunciation such as ours will have to be an act of knowing the denounced reality at the level of alphabetization and postalphabetization, which are in each case cultural action. That is why there is such emphasis on the continual problematization of the learners' existential situations as represented in the codified images. The longer the problematization proceeds, and the more the subjects enter into the "essence" of the problematized object, the more they are able to unveil this essence. The more they unveil it, the more their awakening consciousness deepens, thus leading to the "conscientization" of the situation by the poor classes. Their critical self-insertion into reality, that is, their conscientization, makes the transformation of their state of apathy into the utopian state of *denunciation* and *annunciation* a viable project.

Sowers of the Word

One must not think, however, that learning to read and write precedes conscientization, or vice versa. Conscientization occurs simultaneously with the literacy or postliteracy process. It must be so. In our educational method, the word is not something static or disconnected from men's existential experience, but a dimension of their thought-language about the world. That is why when they participate critically in analyzing the first generative words linked with their existential experience, when they focus on the syllabic families that result from that analysis, when they perceive the mechanism of the syllabic combinations of their language, the learners finally discover, in the various possibilities of combination, their own words. Little by little, as these possibilities multiply, the learners, through mastery of new generative words, expand both their vocabulary and their capacity for expression by the development of their creative imagination.[23]

In some areas in Chile undergoing agrarian reform, the peasants participating in the literacy programs wrote words with their tools on the dirt roads where they were working. They composed the words from the syllabic combinations they were learning. "These men are sowers of the word," said Maria Edi Ferreira, a sociologist from the Santiago team working in the Institute of Training and Research in Agrarian Reform. Indeed, they were not only sowing words but discussing ideas, and coming to understand their role in the world better and better.

We asked one of these sowers of words, finishing the first level of literacy classes, why he hadn't learned to read and write before the agrarian reform.

"Before the agrarian reform, my friend," he said, "I didn't even think. Neither did my friends."

"Why?" we asked.

"Because it wasn't possible. We lived under orders. We only had to carry out orders. We had nothing to say," he replied emphatically.

The simple answer of this peasant is a clear analysis of the culture of silence. In the culture of silence, to exist is only to live. The body carries out orders from above. Thinking is difficult, speaking the word, forbidden.

"When all this land belonged to one *latifundio*," said another man in the same conversation, "there was no reason to read and write. We weren't responsible for anything. The boss gave the orders and we obeyed. Why read and write? Now it's a different story. Take me, for example. In the *asentamiento*, I am responsible not only for my work like all the other men but also for tool repairs.[24] When I started I couldn't read, but I soon realized that I needed to read and write. You can't imagine what it was like to go to Santiago to buy parts. I couldn't get oriented. I was afraid of everything—afraid of the big city, of buying the wrong thing, of being cheated. Now it's all different."

Observe how precisely this peasant described his former experience as an illiterate: his mistrust, his magical (though logical) fear of the world, his timidity. And observe the sense of security with which he repeats, "Now it's all different."

"What did you feel, my friend," we asked another sower of words on a different occasion, "when you were able to write and read your first word?"

"I was happy because I discovered I could make words speak," he replied.

Dario Salas reports, "In our conversations with peasants we were struck by the images they used to express their interest and satisfaction about becoming literate. For example, 'Before we were blind, now the veil has fallen from our eyes'; 'I came only to learn how to sign my name. I never believed I would be able to read, too, at my age'; 'Before, letters seemed like little puppets. Today they say something to me, and I can make them talk.' "[25]

"It is touching," continues Salas, "to observe the delight of the peasants as the world of words opens to them. Sometimes they would say, 'We're so tired our heads ache, but we don't want to leave here without learning to read and write.' "[26]

The following words were taped during research on "generative themes."[27] They are an illiterate's decodification of a codified existential situation.

"You see a house there, sad, as if it were abandoned. When you see a house with a child in it, it seems happier. It gives more joy and peace to people passing by. The father of the family arrives home from work exhausted, worried, bitter, and his little boy comes to meet him with a big hug, because a little boy is not yet like a big person. The father already begins to be happier just from seeing his children. Then he really enjoys himself. He is moved by his son's wanting to please him. The father becomes more peaceful, and forgets his problems."

Note once again the simplicity of expression, both profound and elegant, in the peasant's language. These are the people considered absolutely ignorant by the proponents of the nutritionist concept of literacy.

In 1968, an Uruguayan team published a small book, *You Live as You Can (Se Vive como se puede)*, whose contents are taken from the tape recordings of literacy classes for urban dwellers. Its first edition of three thousand copies was sold out in Montevideo in fifteen days, as was the second edition. The following is an excerpt from this book.

THE COLOR OF WATER

Water? Water? What is water used for?
   "Yes, yes, we saw it (in the picture)."
   "Oh, my native village, so far away. . . ."
   "Do you remember that village?"
   "The stream where I grew up, called Dead Friar . . . you know, I grew up there, a childhood moving from one place to another . . . the color of the water brings back good memories, beautiful memories."
   "What is the water used for?"
   "It is used for washing. We used it to wash clothes, and the animals in the fields used to go there to drink, and we washed ourselves there, too."
   "Did you also use the water for drinking?"
   "Yes, when we were at the stream and had no other water to drink, we drank from the stream. I remember once in 1945 a plague of locusts came from somewhere, and we had to fish them out of the water . . . I was small, but I remember taking out the locusts like this, with my two hands—and I had no others. And I remember how

hot the water was when there was a drought and the stream was almost dry . . . the water was dirty, muddy, and hot, with all kinds of things in it. But we had to drink it or die of thirst."

The whole book is like this, pleasant in style, with great strength of expression of the world of its authors, those anonymous people, sowers of words, seeking to emerge from the culture of silence.

Yes, these ought to be the reading texts for people learning to read and write, and not "Eva saw the grape," "The bird's wing," "If you hammer a nail, be careful not to hit your fingers." Intellectualistic prejudices and above all class prejudices are responsible for the naive and unfounded notions that the people cannot write their own texts, or that a tape of their conversations is valueless, since their conversations are impoverished of meaning. Comparing what the sowers of words said in the above references with what is generally written by specialist authors of reading lessons, we are convinced that only someone with very pronounced lack of taste or a lamentable scientific incompetency would choose the specialists' texts.

Imagine a book written entirely in this simple, poetic, free language of the people, a book on which interdisciplinary teams would collaborate in the spirit of true dialogue. The role of the teams would be to elaborate specialized sections of the book in problematic terms. For example, a section on linguistics would deal simply though not simplistically, with questions fundamental to the learners' critical understanding of language. Let me emphasize again that since one of the important aspects of adult literacy work is the development of the capacity for expression, the section on linguistics would present themes for the learners to discuss, ranging from the increase of vocabulary to questions about communication—including the study of synonyms and antonyms, with its analysis of words in the linguistic context, and the use of metaphor, of which the people are such masters. Another section might provide the tools for a sociological analysis of the content of the texts.

These texts would not, of course, be used for mere mechanical reading, which leaves the readers without any understanding of what is real. Consistent with the nature of this pedagogy, they would become the object of analysis in reading seminars.

Add to all this the great stimulus it would be for those learning to read and write, as well as for students on more advanced levels, to know that they were reading and discussing the work of their own companions.

To undertake such a work, it is necessary to have faith in the people, solidarity with them. It is necessary to be utopian, in the sense in which we have used the word.

NOTES

1. This essay first appeared in the *Harvard Educational Review*, vol. 40, no. 2 (May 1970): 205–225.

2. In languages like Portuguese or Spanish, words are composed syllabically. Thus, every nonmonosyllabic word is, technically, *generative*, in the sense that other words can be constructed from its decomposed syllables. For a word to be authentically generative, however, certain conditions must be present; these will be discussed in a later section of this essay. [At the phonetic level the term *generative word* is properly applicable only in a sound-syllabic reading methodology, while the thematic application is universal. See Sylvia Ashton-Warner's *Teacher* for a different treatment of the concept of generative words at the thematic level.—Editor.]

3. Jean Paul Sartre, *Situations I* (Paris: Librairie Gallimard, 1947), p. 31.

4. The nutritionist concept of knowledge is suggested by "controlled readings," by classes that consist only of lectures; by the use of memorized dialogues in language learning; by bibliographical notes that indicate not only which chapter but which lines and words are to be read; by the methods of evaluating the students' progress in learning.

5. See Paulo Freire, "La alfabetización de adultos, crítica de su visión ingenua; compreensión de su visión crítica," in *Introducción a la acción cultural* (Santiago: ICIRA, 1969).

6. There are two noteworthy exceptions among these primers: (1) In Brazil, *Viver e lutar*, developed by a team of specialists of the Basic Education Movement, sponsored by the National Conference of Bishops. (This reader became the object of controversy after it was banned as subversive by the then governor of Guanabara, Mr. Carlos Lacerda, in 1963.) (2) In Chile, the ESPIGA collection, despite some small defects. The collection was organized by Jefatura de Planes Extraordinarios de Educación de Adultos, of the Public Education Ministry.

7. Since at the time this essay was written the writer did not have access to the primers, and was, therefore, vulnerable to recording phrases imprecisely or to confusing the author of one or another primer, it was thought best not to identify the authors or the titles of the books.

8. The English here would be nonsensical, as is the Portuguese, the point being the emphasis on the consonant *d*.—Editor.

9. The Portuguese word here translated as *marginal men* is *marginado*. This has a passive sense, he who has been made marginal, or sent outside society, as well as the sense of a state of existence on the fringe of society.—Translator.

10. UNESCO: La situación educativa en América Latina, Cuadro no. 20, (Paris, 1960), p. 263.

11. See n. 5.

12. There are two ways to fall into idealism: the one consists of dissolving the real in subjectivity; the other in denying all real subjectivity in the interests of objectivity." Jean Paul Sartre, *Search for a Method*, trans. Hazel E. Barnes (New York: Vintage Books, 1968), p. 33.

13. See Karel Kosik, *Dialéctica de lo concreto* (Mexico: Grijalbo, 1967).

14. *Codification* refers alternatively to the imaging, or the image itself, of some significant aspect of the learner's concrete reality (of a slum dwelling, for example). As such, it becomes both the object of the teacher-learner dialogue and the context for the introduction of the generative word.—Editor.

15. *Decodification* refers to a process of description and interpretation, whether of printed words, pictures, or other "codifications." As such, decodification and decodifying are distinct from the process of decoding, or word recognition.—Editor.

16. On the oppressed consciousness, see Frantz Fanon, *The Wretched of the Earth* (New York: Grove Press, 1968); Albert Memmi, *Colonizer and the Colonized* (New York: Orion Press, 1965); and Paulo Freire, *Pedagogy of the Oppressed* (New York: Seabury Press, 1970).

17. See Fanon, *The Wretched*; Freire, *Pedagogy*.

18. See Louis Althusser, *Pour Marx* (Paris: Librairie François Maspero, 1965); and Paulo Freire, *Annual Report: Activities for 1968, Agrarian Reform, Training and Research Institute ICIRA, Chile*, trans. John Dewitt, Center for the Study of Development and Social Change, Cambridge, Mass., 1969 (mimeographed).

19. We observed in Brazil and Spanish America, especially Chile, that no more than seventeen words were necessary for teaching adults to read and write syllabic languages like Portuguese and Spanish.

20. See Paulo Freire, *Educação como prática da liberdade* (Rio de Janeiro: Paz e Terra, 1967). Chilean edition (Santiago: ICIRA, 1969).

21. On the utopian dimension of denunciation and proclamation, see Leszck Kolakowski, *Toward a Marxist Humanism* (New York: Grove Press, 1969).

22. The right, as a conservative force, needs no utopia; its essence is the

affirmation of existing conditions—a fact and not a utopia—or else the desire to revert to a state which was once an accomplished fact. The right strives to idealize actual conditions, not to change them. What it needs is fraud not utopia." Kolakowski, *Toward a Marxist Humanism*, pp. 71–72.

23. "We have observed that the study of the creative aspect of language use develops the assumption that linguistic and mental process are virtually identical, language providing the primary means for free expansion of thought and feeling, as well as for the functioning of creative imagination." Noam Chomsky, *Cartesian Linguistics* (New York: Harper & Row, 1966), p. 31.

24. After the disappropriation of lands in the agrarian reform in Chile, the peasants who were salaried workers on the large latifundia became "settlers" *(asentados)* during a three-year period in which they received varied assistance from the government through the Agrarian Reform Corporation. This period of "settlement" *(asentamiento)* preceded that of assigning lands to the peasants. This policy is now changing. The phase of settlement of the lands is being abolished, in favor of an immediate distribution of lands to the peasants. The Agrarian Reform Corporation will continue, nevertheless, to aid the peasants.

25. Dario Salas, "Algumas experiências vividas na Supervisão de Educação básica," in *A alfabetização funcional no Chile*. Report to UNESCO (November, 1968).

26. Dario Salas refers here to one of the best adult education programs organized by the Agrarian Reform Corporation in Chile, in strict collaboration with the Ministry of Education and ICIRA. Fifty peasants receive boarding and instruction scholarships for a month. The courses center on discussions of the local, regional, and national situations.

27. An analysis of the objectives and methodology of the investigation of generative themes lies outside the scope of this essay, but is dealt with in the author's *Pedagogy of the Oppressed* (see n. 16).

CHAPTER SEVEN

Cultural Action and Conscientization*

In this chapter I shall consider the philosophical basis and the social context of my own thought.[1] With specific reference to Latin America, I shall discuss the emergence of the masses into the political process in the Third World and analyze the levels of consciousness that characterize that emergence. Finally I shall discuss the nature and function of a truly liberating education in this period of historical transition.

Existence *in* and *with* the World

It is appropriate at this point to make an explicit and systematic analysis of the concept of "conscientization."[2]

*This chapter was translated by Loretta Slover

The starting point for such an analysis must be a critical comprehension of man as a being who exists *in* and *with* the world. Since the basic condition for conscientization is that its agent must be a subject (i.e., a conscious being), conscientization, like education, is specifically and exclusively a human process. It is as conscious beings that men are not only *in* the world but *with* the world, together with other men. Only men, as "open" beings, are able to achieve the complex operation of simultaneously transforming the world by their action and grasping and expressing the world's reality in their creative language.

Men can fulfill the necessary condition of being *with* the world because they are able to gain objective distance from it. Without this objectification, whereby man also objectifies himself, man would be limited to being *in* the world, lacking both self-knowledge and knowledge of the world.

Unlike men, animals are simply *in* the world, incapable of objectifying either themselves or the world. They live a life without time, properly speaking, submerged in life with no possibility of emerging from it, adjusted and adhering to reality. Men, on the contrary, who can sever this adherence and transcend mere being in the world, add to the life they have the existence which they make. To exist is thus a mode of life that is proper to the being who is capable of transforming, of producing, of deciding, of creating, and of communicating himself.

Whereas the being that merely lives is not capable of reflecting upon itself and knowing itself living *in* the world, the existent subject reflects upon his life within the very domain of existence, and questions his relationship to the world. His domain of existence is the domain of work, of history, of culture, of values—the domain in which men experience the dialectic between determinism and freedom.

If they did not sever their adherence to the world and emerge from it as consciousness constituted in the "admiration" of the world as its object, men would be merely determinate beings, and it would be impossible to think in terms of their liberation. Only beings who can reflect upon the fact that they are determined are capable of freeing themselves. Their reflectiveness results not just in a vague and uncommitted awareness but in the exercise of a profoundly transforming action upon the determining reality. "Consciousness of" and "action upon" reality are, therefore, inseparable constituents of the transforming act by which men become beings of relations.[3] By their characteristic reflection, intentionality, temporality, and transcendence, men's consciousness and action are distinct from the mere *contacts* of animals with the world.[4] The animals' contacts are acritical; they do not go beyond the association of sensory images through experience. They are singular and not plural. Animals do not elaborate goals; they exist at the level of immersion and are thus atemporal.

Engagement and objective distance, understanding reality as object, understanding the significance of men's action upon objective reality, creative communication about the object by means of language, plurality of responses to a single challenge—these varied dimensions testify to the existence of critical reflection in men's relationships with the world. Consciousness is constituted in the dialectic of man's objectification of and action upon the world. Yet consciousness is never a mere reflection of but a reflection upon material reality.[5]

If it is true that consciousness is impossible without the world that constitutes it, it is equally true that this world is impossible if the world itself in constituting consciousness does not become an object of its critical reflection. Thus, mechanistic objectivism is just as incapable of explaining men and the world, since it negates men, as is solipsistic idealism, since it negates the world.

For mechanistic objectivism, consciousness is merely a "copy" of objective reality. For solipsism, the world is reduced to a capricious creation of consciousness. In the first case, consciousness would be unable to transcend its conditioning by reality; in the second, insofar as it "creates" reality, it is *a priori* to reality. In either case man is not engaged in transforming reality. That would be impossible in objectivistic terms, because for objectivism, consciousness, the replica or "copy" of reality, is the object of reality, and reality would then be transformed by itself.[6] The solipsistic view is equally incompatible with the concept of transforming reality, since the transformation of an imaginary reality is an absurdity. Thus in both conceptions of consciousness there can be no true praxis. Praxis is only possible where the objective-subjective dialectic is maintained.[7]

Behaviorism also fails to comprehend the dialectic of man-world relationships. Under the form called mechanistic behaviorism, men are negated because they are seen as machines. The second form, logical behaviorism, also negates men, since it affirms that men's consciousness is "merely an abstraction."[8] The process of conscientization cannot be founded upon any of these defective explanations of man-world relationships. Conscientization is viable only because men's consciousness, although conditioned, can recognize that it is conditioned. This "critical" dimension of consciousness accounts for the goals men assign to their transforming acts upon the world. Because they are able to have goals, men alone are capable of entertaining the result of their action even before initiating the proposed action. They are beings who project:

> We presuppose labor in a form that stamps it as exclusively human. A spider conducts operations that resemble those of a weaver, and a bee puts to shame many an architect in the construction of her cells. But what distinguishes the worst architect from the best of the bees is this, that the architect raises his structure in imagination before he erects it in reality.[9]

Although bees, as expert "specialists," can identify the flower they need for making their honey, they do not vary their specialization. They cannot produce byproducts. Their action upon the world is not accompanied by objectification; it lacks the critical reflection that characterizes men's tasks. Whereas animals adapt themselves to the world to survive, men modify the world in order *to be more*. In adapting themselves for the sake of survival, without ends to achieve and choices to make, animals cannot "animalize" the world. "Animalization" of the world would be intimately linked to the "animalization" of animals, and this would presuppose in animals an awareness that they are incomplete, which would engage them in a permanent quest. In fact, however, while they skillfully construct their hives and "manufacture" honey, bees remain bees in their contact with the world; they do not become more or less bees.[10]

For men, as beings of praxis, to transform the world is to humanize it, even if making the world human may not yet signify the humanization of men. It may simply mean impregnating the world with man's curious and inventive presence, imprinting it with the trace of his works. The process of transforming the world, which reveals this presence of man, can lead to his humanization as well as his dehumanization, to his growth or diminution. These alternatives reveal to man his problematic nature and pose a problem for him, requiring that he choose one path or the other. Often this very process of transformation ensnares man and his freedom to choose. Nevertheless, because they impregnate the world with their reflective presence, only men can humanize or dehumanize. Humanization is their utopia, which they announce in denouncing dehumanizing processes.

The reflectiveness and finality of men's relationships with the world would not be possible if these relationships did not occur in an historical as well as physical context. Without critical reflection there is no finality, nor does finality have meaning outside an uninterrupted temporal series of events. For men there is no "here" relative to a "there" that is not connected to a "now," a "before," and an "after." Thus men's relationships with the world are *per se* historical, as are men themselves. Not only do men make the history that makes them, but they can recount the history of this mutual making. In becoming "hominized" in the process of evolution, men become capable of having a biography.[11] Animals, on the contrary, are immersed in a time that belongs not to them but to men.

There is a further fundamental distinction between man's relationships with the world and the animal's contacts with it: only men work. A horse, for example, lacks what is proper to man, what Marx refers to in his example of the bees: "At the end of every labor-process, we get a result that already existed in the imagination of the laborer at its commencement."[12] Action without this dimension is not work. In the fields as well as in the circus, the apparent work of horses reflects the work of men. Action is work not because of the greater or lesser physical effort expended in it by the acting organism, but because of the consciousness the subject has of his own effort, his possibility of programming action, of creating tools and using them to mediate between himself and the object of his action, of having purposes, of anticipating results. Still more, for action to be work, it must result in significant products, which while distinct from the active agent at the same time condition him and become the object of his reflection.[13] As men act upon the world effectively, transforming it by their work, their consciousness is in turn historically and culturally conditioned through the "inversion of praxis." According to the quality of this conditioning, men's consciousness attains various levels in the context of cultural-historical reality. We propose to analyze these levels of consciousness as a further step toward understanding the process of conscientization.

Historical Conditioning and Levels of Consciousness

To understand the levels of consciousness, we must understand cultural-historical reality as a superstructure in relation to an infrastructure. Therefore, we will try to discern, in relative rather than absolute terms, the fundamental characteristics of the historical-cultural configuration to which such levels correspond.

Our intention is not to attempt a study of the origins and historical evolution of consciousness, but to make a concrete introductory analysis of the levels of consciousness in Latin American reality. This does not invalidate such an analysis for other areas of the Third World, nor for those areas in the metropolises that identify themselves with the Third World as "areas of silence."

We will first study the historical-cultural configuration we have called the culture of silence. This mode of culture is a superstructural expression that conditions a special form of consciousness. The culture of silence "overdetermines" the infrastructure in which it originates."[14]

Understanding the culture of silence is possible only if it is taken as a totality that is itself part of a greater whole. In this greater whole we must also recognize the culture or cultures that determine the voice of the culture of silence. We do not mean that the culture of silence is an entity created by the metropolis in specialized laboratories and transported to the Third World. Neither is it true that the culture of silence emerges by spontaneous generation. The fact is that the culture of silence is born in the relationship between the Third World and the metropolis. "It is not the dominator who constructs a culture and imposes it on the dominated. This culture is the result of the structural relations between the dominated and the dominators."[15] Thus, understanding the culture of silence presupposes an analysis of dependence as a relational phenomenon that gives rise to different forms of being, of thinking, of expression, to those of the culture of silence and those of the culture that "has a voice."

We must avoid both of the positions previously criticized in this essay: objectivism, which leads to mechanism, and idealism, which leads to solipsism. Further, we must guard against idealizing the superstructure, dichotomizing it from the infrastructure. If we underestimate either the superstructure or infrastructure it will be impossible to explain the social structure itself. Social structure is not an abstraction; it exists in the dialectic between superstructure and infrastructure. Failing to understand this dialectic, we will not understand the dialectic of change and permanence as the expression of the social structure.

It is true that infrastructure, created in the relations by which the work of man transforms the world, gives rise to superstructure. But it is also true that the latter, mediated by men, who introject its myths, turns upon the infrastructure and "overdetermines" it. If it were not for the dynamic of these precarious relationships in which men exist and work in the world, we could speak neither of social structure, nor of men, nor of a human world.

Let us return to the relationship between the metropolitan society and the dependent society as the source of their respective ways of being, thinking, and expression. Both the metropolitan society and the dependent society, totalities in themselves, are part of a greater whole, the economic, historical, cultural, and political context in which their mutual relationships evolve. Though the context in which these societies relate to each other is the same, the quality of the relationship is obviously different in each case, being determined by the role that each plays in the total context of their interrelation. The action of the metropolitan society upon the dependent society has a directive character, whereas the object society's action, whether it be response or initiative, has a dependent character.

The relationships between the dominator and the dominated reflect the greater social context, even when formally personal. Such relationships imply the introjection by the dominated of the cultural myths of the dominator. Similarly, the dependent society introjects the values and life style of the metropolitan society, since the structure of the latter shapes that of the former. This results in the duality of the dependent society, its ambiguity, its being and not being itself, and the ambivalence characteristic of its long experience of dependency, both attracted by and rejecting the metropolitan society.

The infrastructure of the dependent society is shaped by the director society's will. The resultant superstructure, therefore, reflects the inauthenticity of the infrastructure. Whereas the metropolis can absorb its ideological crises through mechanisms of economic power and a highly developed technology, the dependent structure is too weak to support the slightest popular manifestation. This accounts for the frequent rigidity of the dependent structure.

The dependent society is by definition a silent society. Its voice is not an authentic voice, but merely an echo of the voice of the metropolis—in every way, the metropolis speaks, the dependent society listens.[16]

The silence of the object society in relation to the director society is repeated in the relationships within the object society itself. Its power elites, silent in the face of the metropolis, silence their own people in turn. Only when the people of a dependent society break out of the culture of silence and win their right to speak—only, that is, when radical structural changes transform the dependent society—can such a society as a whole cease to be silent toward the director society.

On the other hand, if a group seizes power through a *coup d'état* and begins to take nationalist economic and cultural defense measures, its policy creates a new contradiction, with one of the following consequences. First, the new regime may exceed its own intentions and be obliged to break definitively with the culture of silence both internally and externally. Or, second, fearing the ascension of the people, it may retrogress, and reimpose silence on the people. Third, the government may sponsor a new type of populism. Stimulated by the first nationalist measures, the submerged masses would have the illusion that they were participating in the transformations of their society, when, in fact, they were being shrewdly manipulated. In Peru, as the military group that took power in 1968 pursued its political objectives, many of its actions caused "cracks" to appear in the most closed areas of Peruvian society. Through these cracks, the masses began to emerge from their silence with increasingly demanding attitudes. Insofar as their demands are met, the masses everywhere tend not only to increase their frequency but also to alter their nature.

Thus, the populist approach also ends up creating serious contradictions for the power group. It finds itself obliged either to break open the culture of silence or to restore it. That is why it seems to us difficult in many parts of the Third World for any government to maintain even a relatively aggressive independent policy toward the metropolis while preserving the culture of silence internally.

In 1961, Jânio Quadros came to power in Brazil in what was perhaps the greatest electoral victory in the nation's history. He attempted to carry out a paradoxical policy of independence toward the metropolis and control over the people. After seven months in office, he unexpectedly announced to the nation that he was obliged to renounce the presidency under pressure from the same hidden forces that had driven President Getulio Vargas to commit suicide. And so he made a melancholy exit and headed for London.

The Brazilian military group that overthrew the Boulart government in 1964, picturesquely designating their action a revolution, followed a coherent course according to our preceding analysis: a consistent policy of servility toward the metropolis and the violent imposition of silence upon their own people. A policy of servility toward the metropolis and rupture of the internal culture of silence would not be viable. Neither would a policy of independence toward the metropolis while maintaining the culture of silence internally.

Latin American societies were established as closed societies from the time of their conquest by the Spanish and Portuguese, when the culture of silence took shape. With the exception of postrevolutionary Cuba, these societies are still closed societies today.[17] They are dependent societies for whom only the poles of decision of which they are the object have changed at different historical moments: Portugal, Spain, England, or the United States.

Latin American societies are closed societies characterized by a rigid hierarchical social structure; by the lack of internal markets, since their economy is controlled from the outside; by the exportation of raw materials and importation of manufactured goods, without a voice in either process; by a precarious and selective educational system whose schools are an instrument of maintaining the status quo; by high percentages of illiteracy and disease, including the naively named "tropical diseases," which are really diseases of underdevelopment and dependence; by alarming rates of infant mortality; by malnutrition, often with irreparable effects on mental faculties; by a low life expectancy; and by a high rate of crime.

There is a mode of consciousness that corresponds to the concrete reality of such dependent societies. It is a consciousness historically conditioned by the social structures. The principal characteristic of this consciousness, as dependent as the society to whose structure it conforms, is its "quasi adherence" to objective reality, or "quasi immersion" in reality.[18] The dominated consciousness does not have sufficient distance from reality to objectify it in order to know it in a critical way.[19] We call this mode of consciousness semi-intransitive.[20]

The Semi-intransitive Consciousness

Semi-intransitive consciousness is typical of closed structures. In its quasi immersion in concrete reality, this consciousness fails to perceive many of reality's challenges, or perceives them in a distorted way. Its semi-intransitiveness is a kind of obliteration imposed by objective conditions. Because of this obliteration, the only data the dominated consciousness grasps are the data that lie within the orbit of its lived experience. This mode of consciousness cannot objectify the facts and problematical situations of daily life. Men whose consciousness exists at this level of quasi immersion lack what we call structural perception, which shapes and reshapes itself from concrete reality in the apprehension of facts and problematical situations. Lacking structural perception, men attribute the sources of such facts and situations in their lives either to some superreality or to something within themselves; in either case to something outside objective reality. It is not hard to trace here the origin of the fatalistic positions men assume in certain situations. If the explanation for those situations lies in a superior power, or in men's own "natural" incapacity, it is obvious that their action will not be orientated toward transforming reality, but toward those superior beings responsible for the problematical situation, or toward that presumed incapacity. Their action, therefore, has the character of defensive magic or therapeutic magic. Thus, before harvest time or sowing, the peasants of the Third World in general perform magical rites, often of a syncretistic religious nature. Even when those rites evolve into cultural traditions, they remain instrumental for a time; the transformation of a magical rite into an expression of tradition does not happen suddenly. It is a process involving, once again, the dialectic between objectivity and subjectivity.[21]

Under the impact of infrastructural changes that produced the first "cracks" in Latin American societies, they entered the present stage of historical and cultural transition—some more intensely than others. In the case of Brazil, this process began with the abolition of slavery at the end of the nineteenth century.[22] It accelerated during World War I and again after the Great Depression, intensified during World War II, and continued with fits and starts to 1964, when the military coup violently returned the nation to silence.

What is important, nevertheless, is that once the cracks in the structure begin to appear, and once societies enter the period of transition, immediately the first movements of emergence of the hitherto submerged and silent masses begin to manifest themselves. This does not mean, however, that movements toward emergence automatically break open the culture of silence. In their relationship to the metropolis, transitional societies continue to be silent totalities. Within them, however, the phenomenon of the emerging masses forces the power elites to experiment with new forms of maintaining the masses in silence, since structural changes that provoke the emergence of the masses also qualitatively alter their quasi-immersed and semi-intransitive consciousness.

The objective datum of a closed society, one of its structural components, is the silence of the masses, a silence broken only by occasional, ineffective rebellions. When this silence coincides with the masses' fatalistic perception of reality, the power elites that impose silence on the masses are rarely questioned.[23] When the closed society begins to crack, however, the new datum becomes the demanding presence of the masses. Silence is no longer seen as an inalterable given, but as the result of a reality that can and must be transformed. This historical transition, lived by Latin American societies to a greater or lesser degree, corresponds to a new phase of popular consciousness, that of "naive transitivity."

The Naive Transitive Consciousness

Formerly the popular consciousness was semi-intransitive, limited to meeting the challenges relative to biological needs. In the process of emerging from silence, the capacity of the popular consciousness expands so that men begin to be able to visualize and distinguish what before was not clearly outlined.

Although the qualitative difference between the semi-intransitive consciousness and the naive transitive consciousness can be explained by the phenomenon of emergence due to structural transformations in society, there are no rigidly defined frontiers between the historical moments that produce qualitative changes in men's awareness. In many respects, the semi-intransitive consciousness remains present in the naive transitive consciousness. In Latin America, for example, almost the entire peasant population is still in the stage of quasi immersion, a stage with a much longer history than the present one of emergence. The semi-intransitive peasant consciousness introjected innumerable myths in the former stage, myths that continue despite a change in awareness toward transitivity. Therefore, the transitive consciousness emerges as a naive consciousness, as dominated as the former. Nevertheless, it is now indisputably more disposed to perceiving the source of its ambiguous existence in the objective conditions of society.

The emergence of the popular consciousness implies, if not the overcoming of the culture of silence, at least the presence of the masses in the historical process applying pressure on the power elite. It can only be understood as one dimension of a more complex phenomenon. That is, the emergence of the popular consciousness, although yet naively intransitive, is also a moment in the developing consciousness of the power elite. In a structure of domination, the silence of the popular masses would not exist but for the power elites who silence them, nor would there be a power elite without the masses. Just as there is a moment of surprise among the masses when they begin to see what they did not see before, there is a corresponding surprise among the elites in power when they find themselves unmasked by the masses. This twofold unveiling provokes anxieties in both the masses and the power elites. The masses become anxious for freedom, anxious to overcome the silence in which they have always existed. The elites are anxious to maintain the status quo by allowing only superficial transformations designed to prevent any real change in their power of prescription.

In the transitional process, the predominantly static character of the "closed society" gradually yields to a dynamism in all dimensions of social life. Contradictions come to the surface, provoking conflicts in which the popular consciousness becomes more and more demanding, causing greater and greater alarm on the part of the elites. As the lines of this historical transition become more sharply etched, illuminating the contradictions inherent in a dependent society, groups of intellectuals and students, who themselves belong to the privileged elite, seek to become engaged in social reality, tending to reject imported schemes and prefabricated solutions. The arts gradually cease to be the mere expression of the easy life of the affluent bourgeoisie, and begin to find their inspiration in the hard life of the people. Poets begin to write about more than their lost loves, and even the theme of lost love becomes less maudlin, more objective and lyrical. They speak now of the field hand and laborer, not as abstract and metaphysical concepts, but as concrete men with concrete lives.[24]

In the case of Brazil, such qualitative changes marked all levels of creative life. As the transitional phase intensified, these active groups focused more and more on their national reality in order to know it better and to create ways of overcoming their society's state of dependency.

The transitional phase also generates a new style of political life, since the old political models of the closed society are no longer adequate where the masses are an emerging historical presence. In the closed society, relations between the elite and the quasi-immersed people are mediated by political bosses, representing the various elitist factions. In Brazil, the invariably paternalistic political bosses are owners not only of their lands but also of the silent and obedient popular masses under their control. Since rural areas in Latin America at first were not touched by the emergence provoked by the cracks in society, they remained predominantly under the control of the political bosses.[25] In urban centers, by contrast, a new kind of leadership emerged to mediate between the power elites and the emerging masses: the populist leadership. There is one characteristic of populist leadership that deserves our particular attention: we refer to its manipulative character.

Although the emergence of the masses from silence does not allow the political style of the formerly closed society to continue, that does not mean that the masses are able to speak on their own behalf. They have merely passed from quasi immersion to a naive transitive state of awareness. Populist leadership thus could be said to be an adequate response to the new presence of the masses in the historical process. But it is a manipulative leadership—manipulative of the masses, since it cannot manipulate the elite.

Populist manipulation of the masses must be seen from two different perspectives. On the one hand, it is undeniably a kind of political opiate that maintains not only the naiveté of the emerging consciousness but also the people's habit of being directed. On the other hand, to the extent that it uses mass protest and demands, political manipulation paradoxically accelerates the process by which the people unveil reality. This paradox sums up the ambiguous character of populism: it is manipulative, yet at the same time a factor in democratic mobilization.[26]

Thus, the new style of political life found in transitional societies is not confined to the manipulative role of its leaders, mediating between the masses and the elites. Indeed, the populist style of political action ends up creating conditions for youth groups and intellectuals to exercise political participation together with the people. Although it is an instance of manipulative paternalism, populism offers the possibility of a critical analysis of the manipulation itself. Within the whole play of contradictions and ambiguities, the emergence of the popular masses in transitional societies prepares the way for the masses to become conscious of their dependent state.

As we have said, the passage of the masses from a semi-intransitive to a naive transitive state of consciousness is also the moment of an awakening consciousness on the part of the elites, a decisive moment for the critical consciousness of progressive groups. At first there appears a fragile awareness among small groups of intellectuals who are still marked by the cultural alienation of society as a whole, an alienation reinforced by their university "formation." As the contradictions typical of a society in transition emerge more clearly, these groups multiply and are able to distinguish more and more precisely what makes up their society. They tend more and more to join with the popular masses in a variety of ways: through literature, plastic arts, the theater, music, education, sports, and folk art. What is important is the communion with the people that some of these groups are able to achieve.

Political Responses to a New Consciousness

At this point the increasingly critical consciousness of these progressive groups, arising from the naive transitivity of the emerging masses, becomes a challenge to the consciousness of the power elites. Societies that find themselves in this historical phase, which cannot be clearly understood outside the critical comprehension of the totality of which they are a part, live in a climate of prerevolution whose dialectical contradiction is the *coup d'état*.

In Latin America, the *coup d'état* has become the answer of the economic and military power elites to the crises of popular emergence. This response varies with the relative influence of the military. According to the degree of its violence and that of the subsequent repression of the people, the *coup d'état* "reactivates" old patterns of behavior in the people, patterns that belong to their former state of quasi immersion. Only this "reactivation" of the culture of silence can explain the passivity of the people when faced with the violence and arbitrary rule of Latin American military coups (with the sole exception of Peru).[27]

It must be emphasized that the *coups d'état* in Latin America are incomprehensible without a dialectical vision of reality; any attempt to understand them mechanistically will lead to a distorted picture. Intensely problematical, unmasking more and more their condition of dependency, Latin American societies in transition are confronted with two contradictory possibilities: revolution or *coup d'état*. The stronger the ideological foundations of a *coup d'état*, the more it is impossible for a society to return afterward to the same political style that created the very conditions for the coup. A *coup d'état* qualitatively alters the process of a society's historical transition, and marks the beginning of a new transition. In the original transitional stage, the coup was the antithetical alternative to revolution; in the new transitional stage, the coup is defined and confirmed as an arbitrary and antipopular power, whose tendency before the continuing possibility of revolution is to become more and more rigid.

In Brazil, the transition marked by the *coup d'état* sets up recapitulation to an ideology of development based on the handing over of the national economy to foreign interests, an ideology in which "the idea of the great international enterprise replaces the idea of the state monopoly as the basis for development."[28] One of the basic requirements for such an ideology is necessarily the silencing of popular sectors and their consequent removal from the sphere of decision making. Popular forces must, therefore, avoid the naive illusion that this transitional stage may afford "openings" that will enable them to reestablish the rhythm of the previous transitional stage, whose political model corresponded to a national populist ideology of development.

The "openings" the new transitional phase offers have their own semantics. Such openings do not signify a return to what has been, but a give-and-take within the play of accommodations demanded by the reigning ideology. Whatever its ideology, the new transitional phase challenges the popular forces to find an entirely new way of proceeding, distinct from their action in the former period when they were contending with the forces those coups brought to power.

One of the reasons for the change is obvious enough. Due to the repression imposed by the coup, the popular forces have to act in silence, and silent action requires a difficult apprenticeship. Further, the popular forces have to search for ways to counter the effects of the reactivation of the culture of silence, which historically engendered the dominated consciousness.

Under these conditions, what is the possibility of survival for the emerging consciousness that has reached the state of naive transitivity? The answer to this question must be found in a deeper analysis of the transitional phase inaugurated by the military coup. Since revolution is still a possibility in this phase, our analysis will focus on the dialectical confrontation between the revolutionary project (or, lamentably, projects) and the new regime.

Cultural Action and Cultural Revolution

It would be unnecessary to tell the revolutionary groups that they are the antagonistic contradiction of the right. But it would not be inexpedient to emphasize that this antagonism, which is born of their opposing purposes, must express itself in a behavior that is equally antagonistic. There ought to be a difference in the praxis of the right and of revolutionary groups that defines them to the people, making the options of each group explicit. This difference between the two groups stems from the utopian nature of the revolutionary groups, and the impossibility of the right to be utopian. This is not an arbitrary distinction, but one that is sufficient to distinguish radically the objectives and forms of action taken by the revolutionary and rightist groups.[29]

To the extent that real utopia implies the denunciation of an unjust reality and the proclamation of a preproject, revolutionary leadership cannot

(a) denounce reality without knowing reality;

    (b) proclaim a new reality without having a draft project that, although it emerges in the denunciation, becomes a viable project only in praxis;

    (c) know reality without relying on the people as well as on objective facts for the source of its knowledge;

    (d) denounce and proclaim by itself;

    (e) make new myths out of the denunciation and annunciation—denunciation and annunciation must be anti-ideological insofar as they result from a scientific knowledge of reality;

    (f) renounce communion with the people, not only during the time between the dialectic of denunciation and annunciation and the concretization of a viable project, but also in the very act of giving that project concrete reality.

Thus, revolutionary leadership falls into internal contradictions that compromise its purpose, when, victim of a fatalist concept of history, it tries to domesticate the people mechanically to a future the leadership knows *a priori*, but thinks the people are incapable of knowing. In this case, revolutionary leadership ceases to be utopian and ends up identified with the right. The right makes no denunciation or proclamation, except, as we have said, to denounce whoever denounces it and to proclaim its own myths.

A true revolutionary project, on the other hand, to which the utopian dimension is natural, is a process in which the people assume the role of subject in the precarious adventure of transforming and recreating the world. The right is necessarily opposed to such a project, and attempts to immobilize it. Thus, to use Erich Fromm's terms, the revolutionary utopia is biophiliac, whereas the right in its rigidity is necrophiliac, as is a revolutionary leadership that has become bureaucratic.[30]

Revolutionary utopia tends to be dynamic rather than static; tends to life rather than death; to the future as a challenge to man's creativity rather than as a repetition of the present; to love as liberation of subjects rather than as pathological possessiveness; to the emotion of life rather than cold abstractions; to living together in harmony rather than gregariousness; to dialogue rather than mutism; to praxis rather than "law and order"; to men who organize themselves reflectively for action rather than men who are organized for passivity; to creative and communicative language rather than prescriptive signals; to reflective challenges rather than domesticating slogans; and to values that are lived rather than myths that are imposed.

The right in its rigidity prefers the dead to the living; the static to the dynamic; the future as a repetition of the past rather than as a creative

venture; pathological forms of love rather than real love; frigid sche-
matization rather than the emotion of living; gregariousness rather than
authentic living together; organization men rather than men who organize;
imposed myths rather than incarnated values; directives rather than
creative and communicative language; and slogans rather than challenges.

It is indispensable for revolutionaries to witness more and more to
the radical difference that separates them from the rightist elite. It is
not enough to condemn the violence of the right, its aristocratic posture,
its myths. Revolutionaries must prove their respect for the people, their
belief and confidence in them, not as a mere strategy but as an implicit
requirement of being a revolutionary. This commitment to the people is
fundamental at any given moment, but especially in the transition period
created by a *coup d'état*.

Victimizing the people by its violence, the coup reimposes, as we
have said, the old climate of the culture of silence. The people, standing
at the threshold of their experience as subjects and participants of society, need signs that will help them recognize who is with them and
who is against them. These signs, or witnesses, are given through projects
proposed by men in dialectic with the structure. Each project constitutes
an interacting totality of objectives, methods, procedures, and techniques. The revolutionary project is distinguished from the rightist project not only by its objectives but also by its total reality. A project's
method cannot be dichotomized from its content and objectives, as if
methods were neutral and equally appropriate for liberation or domination. Such a concept reveals a naive idealism that is satisfied with
the subjective intention of the person who acts.

The revolutionary project is engaged in a struggle against oppressive
and dehumanizing structures. To the extent that it seeks the affirmation
of concrete men as men freeing themselves, any thoughtless concession
to the oppressor's methods is always a danger and a threat to the revolutionary project itself. Revolutionaries must demand of themselves an
imperious coherence. As men, they may make mistakes, they are subject
to equivocation, but they cannot act like reactionaries and call themselves revolutionaries. They must suit their action to historical conditions, taking advantage of the real and unique possibilities that exist.
Their role is to seek the most efficient and viable means of helping the
people to move from the levels of semi-intransitive or naive transitive
consciousness to the level of critical consciousness. This preoccupation,
which alone is authentically liberating, is implicit in the revolutionary

project itself. Originating in the praxis of both the leadership and the rank and file, every revolutionary project is basically "cultural action" in the process of becoming "cultural revolution."

Revolution is a critical process, unrealizable without science and reflection. In the midst of reflective action on the world to be transformed, the people come to recognize that the world is indeed being transformed. The world in transformation is the mediator of the dialogue between the people, at one pole of the act of knowing, and the revolutionary leadership, at the other. If objective conditions do not always permit this dialogue, its existence can be verified by the witness of the leadership.

Che Guevara is an example of the unceasing witness revolutionary leadership gives to dialogue with the people. The more we study his work, the more we perceive his conviction that anyone who wants to become a true revolutionary must be in "communion" with the people. Guevara did not hesitate to recognize the capacity to love as an indispensable condition for authentic revolutionaries. While he constantly noted the failure of the peasants to participate in the guerrilla movement, his references to them in the Bolivian Diary did not express disaffection. He never lost hope of ultimately being able to count on their participation. In the same spirit of communion, Guevara's guerrilla encampment served as the "theoretical context" in which he and his companions together analyzed the concrete events they were living through and planned the strategy of their action.

Guevara did not create dichotomies between the methods, content, and objectives of his projects. In spite of the risks to his and his companions' lives, he justified guerrilla warfare as an introduction to freedom, as a call to life to those who are the living dead. Like Camilo Torres, he became a guerrilla not out of desparation but because, as a lover of men, he dreamt of a new man being born in the experience of liberation. In this sense, Guevara incarnated the authentic revolutionary utopia. He was one of the great prophets of the silent ones of the Third World. Conversant with many of them, he spoke on behalf of all of them.

In citing Guevara and his witness as a guerrilla, we do not mean to say that revolutionaries elsewhere are obliged to repeat the same witness. What is essential is that they strive to achieve communion with the people as he did, patiently and unceasingly. Communion with the people—accessible only to those with a utopian vision, in the sense referred to in this essay—is one of the fundamental characteristics of cultural action for freedom. Authentic communion implies communication between men, mediated by the world. Only praxis in the context of communion makes "conscientization" a viable project. Conscientization is a joint project in that it takes place in a man among other men, men united by their action and by their reflection upon that action and upon the world. Thus men together achieve the state of perceptive clarity that Goldman calls "the maximum of potential consciousness" beyond "real consciousness."[31]

Conscientization is more than a simple *prise de conscience*. While it implies overcoming "false consciousness," overcoming, that is, a semi-intransitive or naive transitive state of consciousness, it implies further the critical insertion of the conscientized person into a demythologized reality. This is why conscientization is an unrealizable project for the right. The right is by its nature incapable of being utopian, and hence it cannot develop a form of cultural action that would bring about conscientization. There can be no conscientization of the people without a radical denunciation of dehumanizing structures, accompanied by the proclamation of a new reality to be created by men. The right cannot unmask itself, nor can it sponsor the means for the people to unmask it more than it is willing to be unmasked. With the increased clarity of the popular consciousness, its own consciousness tends to grow, but this form of conscientization cannot convert itself into a praxis leading to the conscientization of the people. There can be no conscientization without denunciation of unjust structures, a thing that cannot be expected of the right. Nor can there be popular conscientization for domination. The right invents new forms of cultural action only for domination.

Thus, the two forms of cultural action are antagonistic to each other. Whereas cultural action for freedom is characterized by dialogue, and its preeminent purpose is to conscientize the people, cultural action for domination is opposed to dialogue and serves to domesticate the people. The former problematizes, the latter sloganizes.[32] Since cultural action for freedom is committed to the scientific unveiling of reality, to the exposure, that is, of myths and ideologies, it must separate ideology from science. Althusser insists on the necessity of this separation.[33] Cultural action for freedom can be satisfied neither with "the mystifications of ideology," as he calls them, nor with "a simple moral denunciation of myths and errors," but must undertake a "rational and rigorous critique" of ideology. The fundamental role of those committed to cultural action for conscientization is not properly speaking to fabricate the liberating idea but to invite the people to grasp with their minds the truth of their reality.

Consistent with this spirit of knowing, scientific knowledge cannot be knowledge that is merely transmitted, for it would itself become ideological myth, even if it were transmitted with the intention of liberating men. The discrepancy between intention and practice would be resolved in favor of practice. The only authentic points of departure for the scientific knowledge of reality are the dialectical relationships between men and the world, and the critical comprehension of how these relationships are evolved and how they in turn condition men's perception of concrete reality.

Those who use cultural action as a strategy for maintaining their domination over the people have no choice but to indoctrinate the people in a mythified version of reality. In doing so, the right subordinates science and technology to its own ideology, using them to disseminate information and prescriptions in its effort to adjust the people to the reality the "communications" media define as proper. By contrast, for those who undertake cultural action for freedom, science is the indispensable instrument for denouncing the myths created by the right, and philosophy is the matrix of the proclamation of a new reality. Science and philosophy together provide the principles of action for conscientization. Cultural action for conscientization is always a utopian enterprise. That is why it needs philosophy, without which, instead of denouncing reality and announcing the future, it would fall into the "mystifications of ideological knowledge."

The utopian nature of cultural action for freedom is what distinguishes it above all from cultural action for domination. Cultural action for domination, based on myths, cannot pose problems about realilty to the people, nor orient the people to the unveiling of reality, since both of these projects would imply denunciation and annunciation. On the contrary, in problematizing and conscientizing cultural action for freedom, the annunciation of a new reality is the historical project proposed for men's achievement.

In the face of a semi-intransitive or naive transitive state of consciousness among the people, conscientization envisages their attaining critical consciousness, or "the maximum of potential consciousness." This objective cannot terminate when the annunciation becomes concrete. On the contrary, when the annunciation becomes concrete reality, the need becomes even greater for critical consciousness among the people, both horizontally and vertically. Thus, cultural action for freedom, which characterized the movement that struggled for the realization of what was announced, must then transform itself into permanent cultural revolution.

Before going on to elaborate upon the distinct but essentially related moments of cultural action and cultural revolution, let us summarize our preceding points about levels of consciousness. An explicit relationship has been established between cultural action for freedom, conscientization as its chief enterprise, and the transcendence of semi-intransitive and naive transitive states of consciousness by critical consciousness. Critical consciousness is brought about, not through an intellectual effort alone, but through praxis—through the authentic union of action and reflection. Such reflective action cannot be denied to the people. If it were, the people would be no more than activist pawns in the hands of a leadership that reserved for itself the right of decision making. The authentic left cannot fail to stimulate the overcoming of the people's false consciousness, on whatever level it exists, just as the right is incapable of doing so. In order to maintain its power, the right needs an elite who thinks for it, assisting it in accomplishing its projects. Revolutionary leadership needs the people in order to make the revolutionary project a reality, but the people in the process must become more and more critically conscious.

The Continuing Role of Conscientization

After the revolutionary reality is inaugurated, conscientization continues to be indispensable. It is the instrument for ejecting the cultural myths that remain in the people despite the new reality. Further, it is a force countering the bureaucracy, which threatens to deaden the revolutionary vision and dominate the people in the very name of their freedom.[34] Finally, conscientization is a defense against another threat, that of the potential mythicization of the technology that the new society requires to transform its backward infrastructures.[35]

There are two possible directions open to the transitive popular consciousness. The first is growth from a naive state of consciousness to the level of critical consciousness—Goldman's "maximum of potential consciousness." The second is the distortion of the transitive state of consciousness to its pathological form—that of the fanatic or "irrational" consciousness.[36] This form has a mythical character that replaces the magical character of the semi-intransitive and naive transitive states of consciousness. "Massification"—the phenomenon of mass societies—originates at this level. Mass society is not to be associated with the emergence of the masses in the historical process, as an aristocratic eye may view the phenomenon. True, the emergence of the masses with their claims and demands makes them present in the historical process, however naive their consciousness—a phenomenon that accompanies the cracking up of closed societies under the impact of the first infrastructural changes. Mass society, however, occurs much later. It appears in highly technologized, complex societies. In order to function, these societies require specialties, which become specialisms, and rationality, which degenerates into myth-making irrationalism.

Distinct from specialties, to which we are not opposed, specialisms narrow the area of knowledge in such a way that the so-called specialists become generally incapable of thinking. Because they have lost the vision of the whole of which their specialty is only one dimension, they cannot even think correctly in the area of their specialization.

Similarly, the rationality basic to science and technology disappears under the extraordinary effects of technology itself, and its place is taken by myth-making irrationalism. The attempt to explain man as a superior type of robot originates in such irrationalism.[37]

In mass society, ways of thinking become as standardized as ways of dressing and tastes in food. Men begin thinking and acting according to the prescriptions they receive daily from the communications media rather than in response to their dialectical relationships with the world. In mass societies, where everything is prefabricated and behavior is almost automatized, men are lost because they don't have to "risk themselves." They do not have to think about even the smallest things; there is always some manual that says what to do in situation A or B. Rarely do men have to pause at a street corner to think which direction to follow. There's always an arrow that "deproblematizes" the situation. Though street signs are not evil in themselves, and are necessary in cosmopolitan cities, they are among thousands of directional signals in a technological society that, introjected by men, hinder their capacity for critical thinking.

Technology thus ceases to be perceived by men as one of the greatest expressions of their creative power and becomes instead a species of new divinity to which they create a cult of worship. Efficiency ceases to be identified with the power men have to think, to imagine, to risk themselves in creation, and rather comes to mean carrying out orders from above precisely and punctually. [38]

Let it be clear, however, that technological development must be one of the concerns of the revolutionary project. It would be simplistic to attribute responsibility for these deviations to technology in itself.

This would be another kind of irrationalism, that of conceiving of technology as a demonic entity, above and opposed to men. Critically viewed, technology is nothing more nor less than a natural phase of the creative process that engaged man from the moment he forged his first tool and began to transform the world for its humanization.

Considering that technology is not only necessary but also part of man's natural development, the question facing revolutionaries is how to avoid technology's mythical deviations. The techniques of "human relations" are not the answer, for in the final analysis they are only another way of domesticating and alienating men even further in the service of greater productivity. For this and other reasons we have expounded in the course of this essay, we insist on cultural action for freedom. We do not, however, attribute to conscientization any magical power, which would only be to mythicize it. Conscientization is not a magical charm for revolutionaries, but a basic dimension of their reflective action. If men were not "conscious bodies," capable of acting and perceiving, of knowing and re-creating, if they were not conscious of themselves and the world, the idea of conscientization would make no sense—but then, neither would the idea of revolution. Authentic revolutions are undertaken in order to liberate men, precisely because men can know themselves to be oppressed, and be conscious of the oppressive reality in which they exist.

But since, as we have seen, men's consciousness is conditioned by reality, conscientization is first of all the effort to enlighten men about the obstacles preventing them from a clear perception of reality. In this role, conscientization effects the ejection of cultural myths that confuse the people's awareness and make them ambiguous beings.

Because men are historical beings, incomplete and conscious of being incomplete, revolution is as natural and permanent a human dimension as is education. Only a mechanistic mentality holds that education can cease at a certain point, or that revolution can be halted when it attains power. To be authentic, revolution must be a continuous event. Otherwise it will cease to be revolution, and will become sclerotic bureaucracy.

Revolution is always cultural, whether it be in the phase of denouncing an oppressive society and proclaiming the advent of a just society, or in the phase of the new society inaugurated by the revolution. In the new society, the revolutionary process becomes cultural revolution.

Finally, let us clarify the reasons why we have been speaking of cultural action and cultural revolution as distinct moments in the revolutionary process. In the first place, cultural action for freedom is carried out in opposition to the dominating power elite, while cultural revolution takes place in harmony with the revolutionary regime—although this does not mean that it is subordinated to the revolutionary power. All cultural revolution proposes freedom as its goal. Cultural action, on the contrary, if sponsored by the oppressive regime, can be a strategy for domination, in which case it can never become cultural revolution.

The limits of cultural action are set by the oppressive reality itself and by the silence imposed by the power elite. The nature of the oppression, therefore, determines the tactics, which are necessarily different from those employed in cultural revolution. Whereas cultural action for freedom confronts silence both as external fact and introjected reality, cultural revolution confronts it only as introjected reality. Both cultural action for freedom and cultural revolution are an effort to negate the dominating culture culturally, even before the new culture resulting from that negation has become reality. The new cultural reality itself is continuously subject to negation in favor of the increasing affirmation of men. In cultural revolution, however, this negation occurs simultaneously with the birth of the new culture in the womb of the old.

Both cultural action and cultural revolution imply communion between the leaders and the people, as subjects who are transforming reality. In cultural revolution, however, communion is so firm that the leaders and the people become like one body, checked by a permanent process of self-scrutiny.[39] Both cultural action and cultural revolution are founded on scientific knowledge of reality, but in cultural revolution, science is no longer at the service of domination. On two points, however, there is no distinction between cultural action for freedom and cultural revolution. Both are committed to conscientization, and the necessity for each is explained by the "dialectic of overdetermination."

We have spoken of the challenge facing Latin America in this period of historical transition. We believe that other areas of the Third World are no exception to what we have described, though each will present its own particular nuances. If the paths they follow are to lead to liberation, they cannot bypass cultural action for conscientization. Only through such a process can the "maximum of potential consciousness" be attained by the emergent and uncritical masses, and the passage from submersion in semi-intransitiveness to full emergence be achieved. If we have faith in men, we cannot be content with saying that they are human beings while doing nothing concrete so that they may exist as such.

Appendix

We shall describe in this appendix how a generative word from a syllabic language is decomposed, and how new words are formed from it.

Generative word: a trisyllabic word chosen from the "linguistic universe" during research preliminary to the literacy course. Example: *favela* "slum."

Codification: the imaging of a significant aspect of a man's existential situation in a slum. The generative word is inserted in this codification. The codification functions as the knowable object mediating between the knowing subjects—the educator and learners—in the act of knowing they achieve in dialogue.

Real or concrete context: the slum reality as a framework for the objective facts that directly concern slum dwellers.

Theoretical context: the discussion group (*círculo de cultura*), in which the educators and learners—by means of the codification of the objective slum reality—engage in dialogue about the *reason* of the slum reality. The deeper this act of knowing goes, the more reality the learners unveil for what it is, discarding the myths that envelop it. This cognitive operation enables the learners to transform their interpretation of reality from mere opinion to a more critical knowledge.

Thus, as the theoretical context, the discussion group is the specialized environment where we submit the fact found in the concrete context, the slum, to critical analysis. The codification, representing those facts, is the knowable object. Decodification, breaking down the codified totality and putting it together again (retotalizing it), is the process by which the knowing subjects seek to know. The dialogical relationship is indispensable to this act.

Stages of Decodification: there are five stages.

(a) The knowing subjects begin the operation of breaking down the codified whole. This enables them to penetrate the whole in terms of the relationships among its parts, which until then the viewers did not perceive.

(b) After a thorough analysis of the existential situation of the slum, the semantic relation between the generative word and what it signifies is established.

(c) After the word has been seen in the situation, another slide is projected in which only the word appears, without the image of the situation: *favela*.

(d) The generative word is immediately separated into its syllables: *fa ve la*. The "family" of the first syllable is shown:

    fa, fe, fi, fo, fu

Confronted with this syllabic family, the students identify only the syllable *fa*, which they know from the generative word. What is the next step for an educator who believes that learning to read and write is an act of knowing (who also knows that this is not, as for Plato, an act of remembering what has been forgotten)? He realizes that he must supply the students with new information, but he also knows that he must present the material to them as a problem. Thus, he poses two questions:

1. Do these "pieces" (the Brazilian students called the syllables pieces and there was no reason why they should be made to call them syllables) have something that makes them alike and something that makes them different?

After a few moments in which the group looks at the slide in silence, one will say, "They all begin the same way, but they end differently."

2. At this moment, the educator asks another question: If they all begin the same way but end differently, can we call them all *fa?*

Again a brief silence; then, "No!"

Only at this point, having prepared the learners critically for the information, does the educator supply it. Since it was preceded by a problem, the information is not a mere gift.

Then comes the "family" of the word's second syllable:

    va, ve, vi, vo, vu

The educator repeats the process. Some learners immediately say *va, ve, vi, vo, vu*.

The "family" of the third syllable:

    la, le, li, lo, lu

This slide is called the slide of discovery, a phrase coined by Professor Aurenice Cardoso, our assistant when we directed the National Plan for Adult Literacy in Brazil.

The educator proposes a horizontal and a vertical reading of the slide. This strengthens the learners' grasp of the vowel sounds *a, e, i, o, u*.

(e) Next, the educator asks the learners: Do you think we can (never, do you think *you* can) create something with these pieces?

This is the decisive moment for learning. It is the moment when those learning to read and write discover the syllabic composition of words in their language.

After a silence, sometimes disconcerting to the inexperienced educator, the learners begin, one by one, to discover the words of their language by putting together the syllables in a variety of combinations: *favela*, says one, *favo*, another; *fwela; luva; li; vale; vala; viva; falo; fale; fe; fava; vila; lava; vele; vela; vive; vivo; falava*.

With the second generative word, the learners combine its syllables not only among themselves but with those of the first word. Hence, knowing five or six generative words, the learners can begin to write brief notes. At the same time, however, they continue to discuss and critically analyze the real context as represented in the codifications.

This is what the primers cannot do. The authors of primers, as we have pointed out, choose generative words according to their own liking; they themselves decompose them; they themselves recombine their syllables to form new words; and with these words, they themselves evolve the phrases that generally echo the ones we have already quoted: *Eva viu a uva* ("Eva saw the grape"), *A asa é da ave* ("the bird's wing").

NOTES

1. This essay appeared in the *Harvard Educational Review*, vol. 40, no. 3 (August 1970): 452–477. The first two parts of this article also appeared in the May issue of *HER*.

2. Conscientization refers to the process in which men, not as recipients, but as knowing subjects achieve a deepening awareness both of the sociocultural reality that shapes their lives and of their capacity to transform that reality. See chap. 6.—Editor

3. On the distinction between men's relationships and the contacts of animals, see Paulo Freire, *Educação como práctica da liberdade (Rio de Janeiro: Paz e Terra, 1967)*.

4. *Transcendence* in this context signifies the capacity of human consciousness to surpass the limitations of the objective configuration. Without this "transcendental intentionality," consciousness of what exists beyond limitations would be impossible. For example, I am aware of how the table at which I write limits me only because I can transcend its limits, and focus my attention on them.

5. " 'Man, a reasoning animal,' said Aristotle.
'Man, a reflective animal,' let us say more exactly today, putting the accent on the evolutionary characteristics of a quality which signifies the passage from a still diffuse consciousness to one sufficiently well centered to be capable of coinciding with itself. Man not only 'a being who knows' but 'a being who knows he knows.' Possessing *consciousness raised to the power of two* . . . Do we sufficiently feel the radical nature of the difference?" Pierre Teilhard de Chardin, *The Appearance of Man*, trans. J. M. Cohen (New York: Harper & Row, 1965), p.224.

6. Marx rejects the transformation of reality by itself in his third thesis on Feuerbach, *Karl Marx: Selected Writings in Sociology and Social Philosophy*, trans. T. B. Bottomore (New York: McGraw-Hill, 1964), pp.67–68.

7. In a discussion of men-world relationships during a *circulo de cultura*, a Chilean peasant affirmed, "I now see that there is no world without men." When the educator asked, "Suppose all men died, but there were still trees, animals, birds, rivers, and stars, wouldn't this be the world?" "No," replied the peasant, "there would be no one to say, this is the world."

8. We refer to behaviorism as studied in John Beloff's *The Existence of Mind* (New York: Citadel Press, 1964).

9. Karl Marx, *Capital*, ed. Frederick Engels, trans. Samuel Moore and Edward Aveling, (Chicago: Charles H. Kerr, 1932), p. 198.

10. "The tiger does not 'de-tigerize' itself," said Ortega y Gasset in one of his works.

11. See Teilhard de Chardin, *The Appearance of Man*.

12. Karl Marx, *Capital*.

13. This is proper to men's social relations, which imply their relationship to their world. That is why the traditional aristocratic dichotomy between manual work and intellectual work is no more than a myth. All work engages the whole man as an indivisible unity. A factory hand's work can no more be divided into manual or intellectual than ours in writing this essay. The only distinction that can be made between these forms of work is the predominance of the kind of effort demanded by the work: muscular-nervous effort or intellectual effort. Concerning this point, see António Gramsci, *Cultura y literatura* (Madrid: Ediciones Península, 1967), p.31.

14. See Louis Althusser, *Pour Marx* (Paris: Librairie François Maspero, 1965).

15. José Luis Fiori, in a letter to the author. José Luis Fiori was an assistant to the author on his Chilean team in ICIRA, one of the best institutes of its type in the Third World.

16. It is interesting to note how this happens with the churches. The concept of mission lands originates in the metropolis. For a mission land to exist, there must be another that defines it as such. There is a significant coincidence between mission-sending nations and metropolises just as there is between mission lands and the Third World. It would seem to us that, on the contrary, all lands constitute mission territory to the Christian perspective.

17. On "closed societies," see Henri Bergson, *The Two Sources of Morality and Religion*, trans. R. A. Audra and C. Brereton (Garden City, N.Y.: Dou-

bleday, Anchor Books, 1954); and Karl Popper, *The Open Society and Its Enemies* (New York: Harper & Row).

18. This mode of consciousness is still found to be predominant in Latin American rural areas where large property holdings (latifundia) are the rule. The rural areas constitute "closed societies" that maintain the culture of silence intact.

19. See Paulo Freire, *Pedagogy of the Oppressed* (New York: Seabury Press, 1970).

20. See Paulo Freire, *Educação como práctica da liberdade*.

21. It is essential that modernization of backward structures eject the sources of the magic rites that are an integral part of the structures. If not, while it may do away with the phenomenon of magic rites themselves, modernization will proceed to mythologize technology. The myth of technology will replace the magical entities that formerly explained problematical situations. Further, the myth of technology might be seen, not as the substitute for the old forces that in this case continue to exist, but as something superior even to them. Technology would thus be projected as all-powerful, beyond all structures, accessible only to a few privileged men.

22. The abolition of slavery in Brazil brought about the inversion of capital in incipient industries, and stimulated the first waves of German, Italian, and Japanese immigration to the south-central and southern Brazilian states.

23. Although we have not made a precise study of the emergence of black consciousness in the United States, we are tempted to state that, especially in Southern areas, there are divergencies between the younger and older generations that cannot be explained by psychological criteria, but rather by a dialectical understanding of the process of the emerging consciousness. The younger generation, less influenced by fatalism than the older, must logically assume positions qualitatively different from the older generation, not only in regard to passive silence, but also in regard to the methods used by their protest movements.

24. See the excellent study "The Role of Poetry in the Mozambican Revolution," *Africa Today*, vol. 16, no. 2 (April-May 1969).

25. In Latin America, the Mexican, Bolivian, and Cuban revolutions broke open the closed structures of rural areas. Only Cuba, however, succeeded in making this change permanent. Mexico frustrated its revolution, and the Bolivian revolutionary movement was defeated. Nevertheless, the presence of the peasant in the social life of both Mexico and Bolivia is an indisputable fact as a result of that initial opening.

26. Francisco Weffort, in his introduction to Paulo Freire's *Educação como práctica da liberdade*, points out that ambiguity is the principal characteristic of populism. A professor of sociology, Mr. Weffort is one of the best Brazilian analysts of populism today. The Center for the Study of Development and Social Change, Cambridge, Mass., has recently issued a translation of this introduction, by Loretta Slover, for restricted circulation.

27. By the same phenomenon of the people's reversion to silence, Althusser explains how it was possible for the Russian people to put up with the crimes of Stalin's repression.

28. Fernando Henrique Cardoso, "Hegemonia burguesa e independência económica; raízes estruturais da crise política brasileira," *Revista Civilização Brasileira*, no. 17 (January 1968).

29. On re-radicalization and its opposite, sectarianism, see Paulo Freire, *Pedagogy of the Oppressed*.

30. On biophilia and necrophilia, see Erich Fromm, *The Heart of Man* (New York: Harper & Row).

31. Lucien Goldman, *The Human Science and Philosophy* (London: Jonathan Cape, 1969).

32. Paulo Freire, *Pedagogy of the Oppressed*, discusses both these forms of cultural action.

33. Louis Althusser and Etiene Balibar, *Para leer el capital* (Mexico: Siglo XXI, 1969).

34. One must reject the myth that any criticism of necrophilic bureaucracies that swallow up revolutionary proclamation strengthens the right. The opposite is true. Silence, not criticism, in this case would renounce the proclamation and be a capitulation to the right.

35. See Paulo Freire, *Pedagogy of the Oppressed*.

36. See Gabriel Marcel, *Man against Mass Society*, trans. G. S. Fraser (Chicago: A Gateway Edition, 1962).

37. In a recent conversation with the author, the psychoanalyst Michael Maccoby, Dr. Fromm's assistant, stated that his research suggests a relationship between mythologizing technology and necrophilic attitudes.

38. "Professionals who seek self-realization through creative and autonomous behavior without regard to the defined goals, needs, and channels of their respective departments have no more place in a large corporation or government agency than squeamish soldiers in the Army . . . . The social organization of the new Technology, by systematically denying to the general population experiences which are analogous to those of its higher management, contributes very heavily to the growth of social irrationality in our society." John MacDermott, "Technology: The Opiate of Intellectuals," *The New York Review of Books*, no. 2, XIII (July 31, 1969).

39. Even though these statements on cultural revolution can be applied to an analysis of the Chinese cultural revolution and beyond, that is not our intention. We restrict our study to a sketch of the relationship between cultural revolution and cultural action.

CHAPTER EIGHT

The Process of
Political Literacy

W hen I began to write this chapter I looked upon this theme as a challenge. Indeed, seeing this as a challenge forces me to respond critically rather than naively.

My critical attitude in itself presupposes a deep and intimate understanding of the theme in the sense of unveiling it more and more. This essay, then, answers the challenge by becoming yet another challenge for its potential readers. My critical attitude toward this theme leads me into an act of knowledge and this requires not only knowing objects but also a knowing subject, like me.

The Process of Knowing

Since it is always a process, knowing presumes a dialectical situation: not strictly an "I think," but a "we think." It is not the "I think" that constitutes the "we think," but rather the "we think" that makes it possible for me to think.

In epistemological terms, the object of knowledge isn't a term of knowledge for the knowing subject, but mediation of knowledge.

Since this theme is my focus here, it cannot mark the end of my act of knowing. It serves as the appropriate object, establishing a knowing relationship between me and my potential readers as knowing subjects.

I am inviting my readers to act as subjects and thus to reject the idea of merely accepting my analysis.

When writing, I cannot be a pure narrator of something that I take as a given. I have to be critical, just as though I were one of my readers, who in turn should re-create the efforts of my research.

The only difference between my readers and me is that I have to approach this by involving and increasingly centering my curiosity to reach a clearer understanding of our theme, while my readers have to confront both the theme and my understanding of it.

In fact, like any act of study, reading is not just a pastime but a serious task in which readers attempt to clarify the opaque dimensions of their study. To read is to rewrite, not memorize, the contents of what is being read. We need to dispense with the naive idea of "consuming" what we read.

Like Sartre, we might call this artificial notion the nutritionist concept of knowledge, according to which those who read and study do so to become "fat intellectuals."[1] This might justify such expressions as "hungry for knowledge," "thirst for knowledge," and to have or not to have an "appetite for understanding."

This same artificial concept currently informs educational practice in which knowledge is an act of transference. Educators are the possessors of knowledge, whereas learners are "empty vessels" to be filled by the educators' deposits. Hence learners don't have to ask questions or offer any challenge, since their position cannot be other than to receive passively the knowledge their educators deposit.

If knowledge were static and consciousness empty, merely occupying a certain space in the body, this kind of educational practice would be valid. But this is not the case. Knowledge is not something that's made and finished. And consciousness is an "intention" toward the world.

In humanistic terms, knowledge involves a constant unity between action and reflection upon reality. Like our presence in the world, our consciousness transforms knowledge, acting on and thinking about what enables us to reach the stage of reflection. This is precisely why we must take our presence in the world as the focus of our critical analysis. By returning to our previous experiences, we grasp the knowledge of those experiences.

The more we can uncover reasons to explain why we are as we are, the more we can also grasp the reason behind our reality and thus overcome our naive understanding.

This is exactly what we, my readers and I, must do in respect to the theme of this article.

Even as I write, no matter how often readers read what I am writing now, we together must employ a critical analysis, as I have already stated. That is, we must use our experience or that of other subjects in the field as the focus of our reflection, as we attempt to increase our understanding. Then we can begin to understand the real meaning of the language of our theme, "the process of political 'literacy'," where the noun *literacy* appears metaphorically. Given the presence of this metaphor, let's begin our analysis by briefly reviewing the process of adult literacy in terms of linguistics (which in itself is also political), a process upon which the metaphor is based.

Methodologically, this involves the consideration of different practices in the field of adult literacy and presupposes different ways of perceiving illiterates. Two kinds of antagonistic practices that reflect those ways of perceiving illiterates are usually called domesticating and liberating.[2]

After I describe the main characteristics of the domesticating practice in light of my experience in Latin America, I will discuss what I see in the second practice.

Domesticating and Liberating Modes of Education

It is not important whether educators are conscious of following a domesticating practice, since the essential point is the manipulative dimension between educators and learners, by which the latter are made passive objects of action by the former. As passive individuals, learners are not invited to participate creatively in the process of their learning; instead they are "filled" by the educators' words. Within the cultural framework of this practice, educators are presented to the learners as though the latter were separated from life, as though language-thought were possible without reality. In such educational practice, the social structures are never discussed as a problem that needs to be revealed. Quite the contrary, these structures are made obscure by different forms of action that reinforce the learners' "false consciousness."

In any case, in criticizing this practice I think it is necessary to make clear that whether working at the elementary, secondary, or university level or in adult literacy, a self-aware bourgeois educator cannot avoid being engaged in this kind of action.

It would be extremely naive to expect the dominant classes to develop a type of education that would enable subordinate classes to perceive social injustices critically.

This demonstrates that there is no truly neutral education. An ingenuous consciousness, though, might interpret this statement by attributing a lack of neutrality to an educational practice in which educators simply don't respect learners' expressiveness. This is in fact what characterizes the domesticating style of education.

Education of a liberating character is a process by which the educator invites learners to recognize and unveil reality critically. The domestication practice tries to impart a false consciousness to learners, resulting in a facile adaptation to their reality; whereas a liberating practice cannot be reduced to an attempt on the part of the educator to impose freedom on learners.

Although in a domesticating education there is a necessary dichotomy between those who manipulate and those who are manipulated, in an education for freedom there are no subjects who liberate or objects who are liberated, since there is no dichotomy between subject and object.

The domesticating process is in itself prescriptive; the liberating, dialogical.

Education for domestication is an act of transferring "knowledge," whereas education for freedom is an act of knowledge and a process of transforming action that should be exercised on reality.

Adult literacy, seen from a liberating point of view, is an act of knowledge and creativity by which learners function along with educators as knowing subjects. Obviously learners are not seen as "empty vessels," mere recipients of an educator's words.

Since they are not marginal beings who need to be "restored to health" or "saved," learners are viewed as members of the large family of the oppressed. Answers for their situation do not reside in their learning to read alienating stories, but in their making history that will actualize their lives.

If we begin now to consider the problem of political "literacy," our point of departure might be an analysis of political "illiteracy."

From the linguistic point of view, if an illiterate is one who does not know how to read and write, a political illiterate—regardless of whether she or he knows how to read and write—is one who has an ingenuous perception of humanity in its relationships with the world. This person has a naive outlook on social reality, which for this one is a given, that is, social reality is a *fait accompli* rather than something that's still in the making.[3]

One of the political illiterate's tendencies is to escape concrete reality—a way of rejecting it—by losing himself or herself in abstract visions of the world.

Nonetheless, it is impossible for us to escape the real world without critically assuming our presence in it. If we are in the sciences, for instance, we might try to "hide" in what we regard as the neutrality of scientific pursuits, indifferent to how our findings are used, even un-interested in considering for whom or for what interests we are working. Usually when questioned about this, we respond vaguely that we work for the interest of humanity.

If we practice religion, we might establish an unfeasible separation between humanity and transcendence.

If we work in the social sciences, we might treat our society under study as though we are not participants in it. In our celebrated impar-tiality, we might approach this real world as if we were wearing "gloves and masks" in order not to contaminate or be contaminated by it.

Our concept of history can be mechanistic and fatalistic. History is what took place, not what's in the making or what will come. The present is something that should be normalized; whereas the future, as a repetition of the present, becomes the maintenance of the status quo. Sometimes the political illiterate perceives the future, not as a repetition of the present, but as something preestablished, a *fait accompli*. Both views are domesticated visions of the future. The first domesticates the present, which should be repeated; the second reduces the future to something inexorable. Both negate people as beings of praxis, and in so doing they also reject history. They both suffer from a lack of hope.

Experiencing a feeling of impotence before the irrationality of an alienating and almighty reality, the political illiterate tries to find refuge in the false security of subjectivism. Sometimes, instead of refuge, we devote ourselves to "activist" exercises. Perhaps we can compare the political illiterate who has surrendered to these politicized practices with another illiterate, the one who mechanically reads a text without understanding what is being read.

In none of these cases can one appreciate people as a *presence* in the world, as beings of praxis, of action and thinking about the world.

The dichotomy between theory and practice, the universality of a knowledge stripped of its historical-sociological conditioning, the role of philosophy in explaining the world as merely an instrument for our acceptance of the world, education as a pure exposition of facts that transfer abstract values purported to be the inheritance of a pure knowledge—all of these are beliefs proclaimed by the naive consciousness of the political illiterate.

As we become aware of the falseness of these beliefs we find it difficult to appreciate the very impossibility of theory without practice, the impossibility of thinking without a transforming action in the world, as well as the impossibility of knowledge for its own sake or the impossibility of a theory that only explicates reality and offers a neutral education. By contrast, the more refined the political illiterate's naive consciousness, the more stubborn that person will be when facing a critical comprehension of reality.

Education for Political Literacy

Let us now move from analyzing the process of literacy for domestication to discussing generally a few ideas about what education should be doing from a critical point of view, that is, how education, by demystifying reality, can help educators and learners overcome political illiteracy. I will occasionally refer to points previously discussed. I trust that these reiterations, instead of irritating my readers, will help us to better understand our common theme.

I'll begin by restating a basic point: If we don't transcend the idea of education as pure transference of a knowledge that merely describes reality, we will prevent critical consciousness from emerging and thus reinforce political illiteracy.

If our power of choice is really revolutionary, we have to transcend all kinds of education in order to achieve another, one in which to know and to transform reality are reciprocal prerequisites.

The essential point to highlight is transcending a domesticating educational practice for one that is liberating. I stress again that it's impossible in a truly liberating praxis for the educator to follow a domesticating model.

Although the educator in the domesticating model always remains the educator of learners, the educator for freedom has to die, so to speak, as the exclusive educator of learners, that is, as the one educating them. Conversely, the educator must propose to learners that they too die as the exclusive learners of educators so that they can be reborn as real learners—educators of the self-educator and self-learner.

Without this mutual death and rebirth, education for freedom is impossible.

Obviously this does not mean that the educator disappears as though he or she were unnecessary. In rejecting manipulation, I would never accept thoughtless spontaneity.

Whether a reproduction of dominant ideology or a method of achieving revolutionary transforming action, education always requires an educator's presence. There is a radical difference, though, between being present and being the presence itself. Freinet (only one of the great contemporaries in education for freedom) never stopped being present, but he also never exacerbated his presence by transforming his learners' presence into his shadow.

In such a view, at the very moment when she or he begins the process, the educator must be prepared to die as the exclusive educator of the learners. She or he cannot be an educator for freedom if she or he only substitutes the content of another educational practice for a bourgeois practice and thus preserves the form of that practice.[4] In essence, the educator has to live the profound meaning of Easter.

With the exception of at least Cuba and China, one of the tragic mistakes of some socialist societies is their failure to transcend in a profound sense the domesticating character of bourgeois education, an inheritance that amounts to Stalinism.

Thus, socialist education is usually confused with the reduction of Marxist thinking, a thinking that in itself cannot be "confined" within "tablets" to be "prescribed." Accordingly, socialist educators fall into the same "nutritionist" practices that characterize domesticating education.

By perpetuating the school as an instrument for social control and by dichotomizing teaching from learning, educators forget Marx's fundamental warning in his third thesis on Feuerbach: "The educator should also be educated."

Through an education that contradicts its real socialist objectives, these educators instill political illiteracy by making thought antidialectical.

Sometimes perpetuation of the bourgeois ideology is expressed in a strange type of idealism that promises that once the transformation of the bourgeois society is achieved, a "new world" will be automatically created.

In truth, the new world does not surface this way. It comes from that revolutionary process which is permanent and does not diminish when the revolution achieves power. The creation of this new world, which should never be made "sacred," requires the conscious participation of all the people, the transcendence of the dichotomy between manual and intellectual labor, and a form of education that does not reproduce the bourgeoisie.

One of the great merits of the Chinese Cultural Revolution was its rejection of static, antidialectical, or overconservative concepts of China's history. Here there seems to be a permanent mobilization of the people in the sense of consciously creating and re-creating society. In China, to be conscious is not a slogan or a ready-made idea. To be conscious is a radical way of being, a way characteristic of humanity.

The Process of Conscientization

To avoid possible misunderstandings let me make clear that up to now I have been referring to the role of consciousness in the liberating practice.

In a dialectical position, it is impossible for me to accept the ingenuous separation between consciousness and the world. When we do that, we fall into either illusions of idealism or mechanistic errors.[5]

The word conscientization (based on the Brazilian *conscientização*), the process by which human beings participate critically in a transforming act, should not be understood as an idealist manipulation. Even if our vision in conscientization is dialogical, not subjective or mechanistic, we cannot attribute to this consciousness a role that it does not have, that of transforming reality. Yet we also must not reduce consciousness to a mere reflection of reality.

One of the important points in conscientization is to provoke recognition of the world, not as a "given" world, but as a world dynamically "in the making."

Conscientization thus involves a constant clarification of what remains hidden within us while we move about in the world, though we are not necessarily regarding the world as the object of our critical reflection.[6]

I know very well that implied in this critical reflection about the real world as something made and an unveiling of yet another reality, conscientization cannot ignore the transforming action that produces this unveiling and concrete realization. Again, I know very well that to simply substitute an ingenuous perception of reality for a critical one, it's sufficient for the oppressed to liberate themselves. To do so, they need to organize in a revolutionary manner and to transform the real world in a revolutionary manner. This sense of organization requires a conscious action, making clear what's unclear in the profound vision of consciousness.

It is precisely this creation of a new reality, prefigured in the revolutionary criticism of the old one, that cannot exhaust the conscientization process, a process as permanent as any real revolution.

As transforming beings, people may stay "glued" to the new reality that comes about from their action, but they will be submerged in a new "unclear" vision.

Conscientization, which occurs as a process at any given moment, should continue whenever and wherever the transformed reality assumes a new face.

Notes

1. Jean Paul Sartre, *Situations I* (Paris: Librairie Gallimard, 1959).

2. This does not mean, though, that by the mere fact of developing such a practice it will be enough to liberate the oppressed. Rather, it means that such a practice aids liberation to the extent that it contributes to illiterates' understanding of their reality in critical terms.

3. In this sense, many illiterates and semi-illiterates are from a linguistic point of view actual political literates, much more so than certain erudite literates. This isn't surprising. The political practices of the former, their experiences through conflict (in essence, the midwife of real consciousness), teach them what the erudite don't or can't learn from books.

4. I don't think it is necessay to emphasize why such educational practice

is not encouraged by the dominant classes. Nevertheless, it's lamentable that this practice doesn't occur in a revolutionary society or that it is not employed by revolutionary movements in their efforts to organize the dominated classes.

5. "There are two ways to fall into idealism: one consists of dissolving the real insubjectivity; the other, in denying all real subjectivity in the interests of objectivity." Jean Paul Sartre, *Search for a Method*, trans., Hazel E. Barnes (New York: Vintage Books, 1968), p. 33.

6. On this subject see Karel Kosik, *Dialéctica de lo concreto* (Mexico: Grijalbo, 1976).

CHAPTER NINE

Humanistic Education

The theme of an essay is not merely what appears on the surface in words. There is always something hidden, something with a deeper meaning that is the key for complete understanding. Accordingly, whenever possible, writing on or toward real issues entails an extensive effort to see through deceiving appearances that may blur our vision. Often we have to surmount a number of difficulties in disentangling the issues from these appearances so that we can perceive the total theme as an actual phenomenon in an actual world.

To do this, we address our theme through the richness of its network of specific characteristics that are sometimes not obvious. The more we are able to penetrate this network, though, the more we are able to capture the overall theme in its complex dynamism.

Realizing a Theme

The process of writing on a particular theme is not just a narrative act. In perceiving the theme as a phenomenon that takes place in a concrete reality and that mediates men and women, we writers must assume a gnosiological attitude.

In the same ways, readers in assuming a similar attitude have to remake our gnosiological efforts. Readers should not be simple clients of the gnosiological act of the writer. In brief, both need to avoid the Socratic error of regarding the definition of a concept as knowledge of the thing defined.

What we must not do is overdefine the concept of the theme, or even take what it involves as a given fact; nor should we simply describe it or explain it. To the contrary, we should assume a committed attitude toward our theme, an attitude of one who does not want merely to describe what goes on as it happens. We want, above all, to transform the real world of our theme so that whatever might be happening now can be changed later.

In our getting to know the real world as it is, however, this committed attitude toward the issues in our theme does not defend our harboring preconceptions, that is, preconceptions that might distort and ultimately slant the facts to our benefit.

In trying scientifically to know the reality where our theme originates, we should not only submit our epistemological procedures to our version of "the truth" but also search for the truth based on facts. While we engage in the scientific research of reality, though, we must not assume a neutral attitude. We can't confuse our preoccupation with the truth (characteristic of any serious scientific effort) with so-called scientific neutrality, which in fact does not exist.

Our committed, but nonneutral attitude toward the reality we are trying to know must first render knowledge as a process involving an action and reflection of man in the world. By virtue of the teleological character in the unity of action and reflection (that is, of praxis), by which a man or woman who transforms the world is transformed, he or she cannot discard this attitude of commitment that, in turn, preserves his or her critical spirit and scientism. We cannot remain ethically indifferent to the fate that may be imposed on our findings by those who have the power of decisions, but merely yield to science and its interests and subsequently dictate their aims to the majority.

On the other hand, our attitude of commitment to these issues is further justified by the fact that every theme has its counterargument or opposing theme with goals to be met, and, of course, the greater the antagonism between these sets of goals, the more contrary will be their respective themes. Thus while we delve into and reveal our understanding of a theme, we also reveal its counterpart, giving us a choice that in turn demands that we commit ourselves to a form of action consonant with the goals implicit in the theme. Again, while we need to be efficient in performing these tasks, we should not commit ourselves to a type of action that benefits the opposing theme. The more we get to know the sociohistorical reality of the issues in our themes, in their dialectical relation with opposing issues, the more impossible it will be for us to remain neutral. Since proclaimed neutrality always involves a hidden choice, we insist that these themes, while historical, incorporate human values and orientations in human experience.

When we critically approach this process and recognize it as a theme, we are forced to apprehend this, not as an abstract ideal, but as a historical challenge, contrary to the dehumanization of our own objective reality. Dehumanization and humanistic education cannot occur outside the history of men and women, outside the very social structures that we have created and to which we are conditioned.

Contrasting Modes of Education

Dehumanization is a concrete expression of alienation and domination; humanistic education is a utopian project of the dominated and oppressed. Obviously both imply action by people in a social reality—the first, in the sense of preserving the status quo, the second in a radical transformation of the oppressor's world.

It seems important here to emphasize what is most obvious—the interrelationship of dehumanization and humanistic education. Again, both require action from men and women to maintain or modify their respective realities. We emphasize this to overcome idealist illusions and pipe dreams of an eventual humanistic education for mankind without the necessary transformation of an oppressed and unjust world. Such a dream actually serves the interests of the advantaged and readily exposes an ideology that concretizes the welfare syndrome by urging the oppressed to wait patiently for those sunnier days, delayed for now, but soon to appear.

There is no humanistic dimension in oppression, nor is there dehumanization in true liberation. But liberation doesn't take hold of people's consciousness if they are isolated from the world. Liberation occurs in their historical praxis when it involves a critical consciousness of the implicit relationship of consciousness and world.

This is one of the fundamental points of the pedagogical implications of the humanistic process that lead us to another impossibility underscored in various studies: the so-called neutrality of education. Just as the struggle for humanistic education presupposes the threat of, or actual, dehumanization, the same struggle also implies opposing educational practices. As opposites, the humanistic process and dehumanization assign educational tasks that are necessarily antagonistic as well. The educator who has made a humanistic and, therefore, liberating choice is less apt to be committed to preconceptions and, accordingly, in his or her own practice will be able to appreciate the dialectical relation of consciousness and world or man and world.

In essence, one of the radical differences between education as a dominating and dehumanizing task and education as a humanistic and liberating task is that the former is a pure act of transference of knowledge, whereas the latter is an act of knowledge. As expected, both these radically opposite tasks, which also require opposing procedures, revolve around the relation between consciousness and world.

In its relation to consciousness and world, education as a dominating task assumes that consciousness is and should be merely an empty receptacle to be "filled"; education as a liberating and humanistic task views consciousness as "intention" toward the world.

In the case of dominating education, the captor of existing knowledge negates the active principle of consciousness. This form of education involves practices by which one strives to "domesticate" consciousness, transforming it, as we have said, into an empty receptacle. Education in cultural action for domination is reduced to a situation in which the educator as "the one who knows" transfers existing knowledge to the learner as "the one who does not know."

In a humanistic form of education, once we verify our inquisitive nature as researchers and investigators of reflexive (and not merely reflective) consciousness, and once we make that knowledge accessible, we automatically ascertain our capacity to recognize or to remake existing knowledge. Moreover, we can identify and appreciate what is still unknown. If this weren't so, that is, if the type of consciousness that recognizes existing knowledge could not keep searching for new knowledge, there would be no way to explicate today's knowledge. Since knowing is a process, knowledge that exists today was once only a viability and it then became a new knowledge, relative and therefore successive to yesterday's existing knowledge.

Instead of being an alienating transference of knowledge, education or cultural action for freedom is the authentication of knowledge by which learners and educators as "consciousness" or as ones filled with "intention" join in the quest for new knowledge as a consequence of their apprehending existing knowledge. But, again, if education as a practice of freedom is to achieve this understanding of existing knowledge in the search for new knowledge, it can never do so by "treating" consciousness in the same way dominating education "treats"it. The educator who makes a humanistic choice must correctly perceive the relationship between consciousness and world, and man and world. A liberating form of educational practice by definition proposes an "archaeology" of consciousness. Through their own efforts people can remake the natural path where consciousness emerges as the capacity for self-perception. In the act of *hominização*, in which reflection establishes itself, one sees the "individual and instantaneous leap from instinct to thought."[1] This is so because at that very remote moment the reflective consciousness characterized a human as an animal capable not only of knowing but also of knowing himself or herself in the process of knowing. Thus, consciousness emerges as "intention" and not just as a receptacle to be filled.

This critical perception obliterates the simplistic dualism that establishes a nonexistent dichotomy between consciousness and the world. On the other hand, it corrects the mistaken notions that breed naive consciousness, ideologized in the structures of domination such as the perception of consciousness as an empty receptacle.

The more "anaesthetized" men are in their reflective power, which they acquired in their evolution and which now fundamentally distinguishes them from animals, the more obstacles they find in the process of truly liberating themselves.[2] It's crucial for a dehumanizing ideology to avoid, at all costs, any opportunity for men and women to perceive themselves as reflective, active beings, as creators and transformers of the world. Indeed, it is in the interest of this ideology to formalize domesticated consciousness in terms of an empty receptacle.

Before acting on and fulfilling their objectives, the dominant classes must confront one obstacle they have been attempting to overcome with increasing efficiency through the science and technology at their disposal: since they are unable to eliminate the human capacity to think, they obscure the real world by a conditioned and specious reasoning about people and the world in general.

This mystification of reality consists of making the world appear different from what it is and, in the process and by necessity, of imparting an artificial consciousness. In fact, it would be impossible to falsify the real world, as the real world of consciousness, without falsifying the consciousness of the real world. One does not exist without the other.

In any case, a process of liberation involves that "archaeology" of consciousness through which, as we have said, man constructs a natural path through which consciousness emerges with an ability to perceive itself: whereas in the process of domination, mystification presupposes the development of "irrationality." This nevertheless does not mean returning to a way of life that's simply instinctive or a distortion of reason. The mythical element introduced here does not actually forbid people to think; rather it makes the critical application of their thinking difficult by affording people the illusion that they think correctly. Propaganda establishes itself, then, as an efficient instrument for legitimizing this illusion, and through it the dominant classes not only proclaim the "excellent" quality of the social order but also impugn any expression of indignation toward the social order as "subversive and dangerous to the common welfare." Thus, mystification leads to the "sacredness" of the social order, untouchable, undiscussable. Any who question the social order must be punished one way or another, and they are labeled by similar means of propaganda as "bad citizens in the service of the international demon."[3]

Society and Education

It is characteristic of the permanent search for humanistic education that the more you have freedom to criticize, the more necessary is the sacredness of the domesticating social order for its self-preservation. For this reason, all attempts at mystification obviously tend to become totalitarian, that is, they tend to reach all human endeavors. No category or enterprise can escape falsification, because any exception might become a threat to the sacredness of the established order. In this sense, schooling at whatever level plays one of the most vital roles, as an efficient mechanism for social control. It is not hard to find educators whose idea of education is "to adapt the learner to his environment," and as a rule formal education has not been doing much more than this.

Generally speaking, the good student is not one who is restless or intractable, or one who reveals one's doubts or wants to know the reason behind facts, or one who breaks with preestablished models, or one who denounces a mediocre bureaucracy, or one who refuses to be an object. To the contrary, the so-called good student is one who repeats, who renounces critical thinking, who adjusts to models, and who "thinks it pretty to be a rhinoceros."[4]

On the other hand, the teacher who makes himself or herself "divine," as sacred as the sacredness of the school, appears most often as an untouchable, literally and figuratively. A student may not even put a hand on the teacher's shoulder as a gesture of affection. This intimacy of mortals would threaten the necessary distance between teacher and students—students, after all, should do nothing other than receive the contents that the educator transfers to them, contents that are impregnated with the ideological character vital to the interests of the sacred order.

What did you learn in school today, dear little boy of mine?
What did you learn in school today, dear little boy of mine?

I learned that Washington never told a lie,
I learned that soldiers seldom die,
I learned that everybody's free,
And that's what the teacher said to me.

That's what I learned in school today,
That's what I learned in school.

I learned that policemen are my friends,
I learned that justice never ends,
I learned that murderers die for their crimes
Even if we make a mistake sometimes.

I learned our government must be strong,
It's always right and never wrong
Our leaders are the finest men
And we elect them again and again.

I learned that war is not so bad,
I learned about the great ones we have had,
We've fought in Germany and in France,
And someday I may get my chance.

That's what I learned in school today,
That's what I learned in school.[5]

With one or two variations, this might very well be the song that millions of children from different parts of the world would sing if we were to ask them what they learned in school today.

Yet if we expand our curiosity and begin to ask students what they learned at the university today, their responses will not be dramatically different from that of the child in Tom Paxton's song. Among other things, they might say:

> Today at the university we learned that objectivity in science requires neutrality on the part of the scientist; we learned today that knowledge is pure, universal, and unconditional and that the university is the site of this knowledge. We learned today, although only tacitly, that the world is divided between those who know and those who don't (that is, those who do manual work) and the university is the home of the former. We learned today that the university is a temple of pure knowledge and that it has to soar above earthly preoccupations, such as mankind's liberation.
>
> We learned today that reality is a given, that it is our scientific impartiality that allows us to describe it somewhat as it is. Since we have described it as it is, we don't have to investigate the principal reasons that would explain it as it is. But if we should try to denounce the real world as it is by proclaiming a new way of living, we learned at the university today that we would no longer be scientists, but ideologues.
>
> We learned today that economic development is a purely technical problem, that the underdeveloped peoples are incapable (sometimes because of their mixed blood, their nature, or climatic reasons).
>
> We were informed that blacks learn less than whites because they are genetically inferior, even when they demonstrate unquestionable capacities, for example, dancing, dexterity, and enduring heavy physical labor.

Whether through schooling or otherwise, what is indisputable is that all this mystification winds up as an obstacle to people's critical capacity, thus favoring the preservation of the status quo.

The internalization of these myths, along with many others, explains the contradiction between forms of action and actual choices made by many people.

Many speak in reference to the human being and this human being becomes fossilized in a banal phrase because they don't recognize the human dimension in those very men who are dominated as objects.

Many claim to be committed to the cause of liberation, but they conform to those very myths that negate humanistic acts.

Many analyze social mechanisms of oppression and simultaneously, through equally repressive means, they hold back the students they are lecturing.

Many declare they are revolutionaries, but they don't trust the oppressed whom they pretend to liberate, as though this weren't an aberrant contradiction.

Many want a humanistic education, yet they also want to maintain the social reality in which people find themselves dehumanized.

In brief, they fear liberation. And in fearing liberation, they dare not risk constructing it in a brotherhood with those who are deprived of freedom.

Notes

1. Pierre Teilhard de Chardin, *El Fenómeno humano* (Madrid:Taurus. 1963), p.218.

2. We don't want to say that a simple reflective capacity is sufficient for liberation. It's clear that liberation requires a transforming act upon the objective, oppressive, and thus dehumanized reality. Yet since there is no authentic reflection without action and vice versa, in the end they both constitute in an undichotomized sense the real praxis of men in the world, without which liberation is impossible.

3. Punishment varies depending on the degree of opposition from those refusing to adjust to the domestication imposed by the oppressive order.

4. See Eugène Ionesco, *Rhinoceros*.

5. Tom Paxton, sung by Pete Seeger.

CHAPTER TEN

Education, Liberation and the Church

W e begin with an affirmation; though almost a truism, it clearly sets forth our position on the present subject.[1] We cannot discuss churches, education, or the role of the churches in education other than historically. Churches are not abstract entities; they are institutions involved in history. Therefore to understand their educational role we must take into consideration the concrete situation in which they exist.

The moment these statements are taken seriously, we can no longer speak of the neutrality of the churches or the neutrality of education. Such assertions of neutrality must be judged as coming either from those who have a totally naive view of the church and history or from those who shrewdly mask a realistic understanding behind a claim of neutrality. Objectively, nevertheless, both groups fit into the same ideological perspective. When they insist on the neutrality of the church in relation to history or to political action, they take political stands that inevitably favor the power elites against the masses. "Washing one's hands" of the conflict between the powerful and the powerless means to side with the powerful, not to be neutral.

Alongside the neutral attitude, there are more subtle and more attractive means of serving the interests of the powerful while appearing to favor the oppressed. Here again we find the naive and the shrewd walking hand in hand. I refer again to what we might call anaesthetic or aspirin practices, expressions of a subjectivist idealism that can only lead to the preservation of the status quo. In the last analysis the basic presupposition of such action is the illusion that the hearts of men and women can be transformed while the social structures that make those hearts "sick" are left intact and unchanged.

The illusion that suggests it is possible, by means of sermons, humanitarian works, and the encouragement of otherworldly values, to change men's consciousness and thereby transform the world exists only in those we term naive (or moralistic as Niebuhr would have said).[2] The shrewd are well aware that such action can slow down the basic process of radical change in social structures. This radical change is a precondition for the awakening of consciousness, and the process is neither automatic nor mechanical.

Although, objectively, both groups are equally ineffectual in producing liberation or the real humanization of human beings, there is still a basic difference between them, which should be underlined. Both are caught up in the ideology of the ruling social class, but the shrewd consciously accept this ideology as their own. The naive, in the first instance unconscious of their true position, can through their action come to take the ideology of domination for their own and, in the process, move from naiveté to shrewdness. They can also come to renounce their idealistic illusions altogether, forsaking their uncritical adherence to the ruling class. In committing themselves to the oppressed, they begin a new period of apprenticeship. This is not, however, to say that their commitment to the oppressed is thereby finally sealed. It will be severely tested during the course of this new apprenticeship when confronted, in a more serious and profound way than ever before, with the hazardous nature of existence. To pass such a test is not easy.

This new apprenticeship will violently break down the elitist concept of existence they had absorbed while being ideologized. The *sine qua non* the apprenticeship demands is that, first of all, they really experience their own Easter, that they die as elitists so as to be resurrected on the side of the oppressed, that they be born again with the beings who were not allowed to be. Such a process implies a renunciation of myths that are dear to them: the myth of their superiority, of their purity of soul, of their virtues, their wisdom, the myth that they save the poor, the myth of the neutrality of the church, of theology, education, science, technology, the myth of their own impartiality. From these grow the other myths: of the inferiority of other people, of their spiritual and physical impurity, and of the absolute ignorance of the oppressed.

This Easter, which results in the changing of consciousness, must be existentially experienced. The real Easter is not commemorative rhetoric. It is praxis; it is historical involvement. The old Easter of rhetoric is dead—with no hope of resurrection. It is only in the authenticity of historical praxis that Easter becomes the death that makes life possible. But the bourgeois world view, basically necrophiliac (death-loving) and therefore static, is unable to accept this supremely biophiliac (life-loving) experience of Easter. The bourgeois mentality—which is far more than just a convenient abstraction—kills the profound historical dynamism of Easter and turns it into no more than a date on the calendar.

The lust to possess, a sign of the necrophiliac world view, rejects the deeper meaning of resurrection.[3] Why should I be interested in rebirth if I hold in my hands, as objects to be possessed, the torn body and soul of the oppressed? I can only experience rebirth at the side of the oppressed by being born again, with them, in the process of liberation. I cannot turn such a rebirth into a means of *owning* the world, since it is essentially a means of *transforming* the world.

If those who were once naive continue their new apprenticeship, they will come to understand that consciousness is not changed by lessons, lectures, and eloquent sermons but by the action of human beings on the world. Consciousness does not arbitrarily create reality, as they thought in their old naive days of subjectivist idealism.

Conscientization

They will also discover to what extent their idealism had confused any number of concepts—for example, "conscientization," which is so badly understood—when they tried to offer magic remedies for healing the hearts of mankind without changing the social structures, or, equally idealistic, when they claimed that conscientization was a similarly magic means of reconciling the irreconcilable.

Conscientization appeared to them then as a sort of third way that would allow them to escape miraculously from the problems of class conflict, creating through mutual understanding a world of peace and harmony between oppressor and oppressed. When both were conscientized there would be neither oppressor nor oppressed, for all would love each other as brothers, and differences would be resolved through round-table discussions—or over a good whiskey.

Basically, this idealistic vision, which works only for the oppressors, is exactly the position that Niebuhr vehemently condemned as moralistic, whether it be found in the religious or the secular domain.[4]

Such mythologizing of conscientization, be it in Latin America or elsewhere, be it at the hands of the shrewd or the naive, constitutes an obstacle rather than an aid to the liberation process. It becomes, on the one hand, an obstacle because in emptying conscientization of its dialectical content and thus making it into a panacea, it puts it, as we have seen, at the service of the oppressors. On the other hand, it creates an obstacle because such idealistic disfiguration leads many Latin American groups, especially among youth, to fall into the opposite error of mechanical objectivism. In reacting against the alienating subjectivism that causes this distortion, they end up by denying the role of consciousness in the transformation of reality and therefore also denying the dialectical union between consciousness and the world. They no longer see the difference between such things as class consciousness and the consciousness of class needs.[5] Between the two there is a sort of dialectical gap that must be bridged. Neither subjectivism nor mechanical objectivism is able to do this.

These groups are right in affirming, as do we, that one cannot change consciousness outside of praxis. But it must be emphasized that the praxis by which consciousness is changed is not only action but action *and* reflection. Thus there is a unity between practice and theory in which both are constructed, shaped, and reshaped in constant movement from practice to theory, then back to a new practice.

Theoretical praxis is what occurs when we step back from accomplished praxis (or from praxis that is being accomplished) in order to see it more clearly. Thus, theoretical praxis is only authentic when it maintains the dialectical movement between itself and that praxis which will be carried out in a particular context. These two forms of praxis are two inseparable moments of the process by which we reach critical understanding. In other words, reflection is only real when it sends us back, as Sartre insists, to the given situation in which we act.

Hence conscientization, whether or not associated with literacy training, must be a critical attempt to reveal reality, not just alienating small talk. It must, that is, be related to political involvement. There is no conscientization if the result is not the conscious action of the oppressed as an exploited social class, struggling for liberation.[6] What is more, no one conscientizes anyone else. The educator and the people together conscientize themselves, thanks to the dialectical movement that relates critical reflection on past action to the continuing struggle.

Education for Liberation

Another dimension of the mythologizing of conscientization—whether by the shrewd or the naive—is their attempt to convert the well-known education for liberation into a purely methodological problem, considering methods as something purely neutral. This removes—or pretends to remove—all political content from education, so that the expression *education for liberation* no longer means anything.

Actually, insofar as this type of education is reduced to methods and techniques by which students and educators look at social reality—when they do look at it—only to describe it, this education becomes as domesticating as any other. Education for liberation does not merely free students from blackboards just to offer them projectors.[7] On the contrary, it is concerned, as a social praxis, with helping to free human beings from the oppression that strangles them in their objective reality. It is therefore political education, just as political as the education that claims to be neutral, although actually serving the power elite. It is thus a form of education that can only be put into practice systematically when society is radically transformed.[8] Only the "innocent" could possibly think that the power elite would encourage a type of education that denounces them even more clearly than do all the contradictions of their power structures.[9] Such naiveté also reveals a dangerous underestimation of the capacity and audacity of the elite. Truly liberating education can only be put into practice outside the ordinary system, and even then with great cautiousness, by those who overcome their naiveté and commit themselves to authentic liberation.

A growing number of Christians in Latin America are discovering these things and finding themselves forced to take sides: either to change their naiveté into shrewdness and consciously align themselves with the ideology of domination or to join forces with the oppressed and in full identification with them seek true liberation. We have already stated that if they renounce their uncritical adherence to the dominant classes, their new apprenticeship with the people presents a challenge; in meeting this challenge they encounter risks formerly unknown.

During what we are calling their new apprenticeship, many Christians soon realize that previously when they had engaged in purely palliative action—whether social or religious (for example, fervent support of maxims such as "The family that prays together stays together")—they were praised for their Christian virtues. They now begin to realize, however, that the family that prays together also needs a house, employment, bread, clothing, health, and education for their children, that they need to express themselves and their world by creating and recreating it, that their bodies, souls, and dignity must be respected if they are to stay together in more than suffering and misery.[10] When they begin to see all this, they find their very faith being called into question by those who wish to have even more political, economic, and ecclesiastical power for the reshaping of the consciousness of others.

As their new apprenticeship begins to show more clearly the dramatic situation in which they live and which leads them to undertake action that is less paternalistic, they come to be seen as diabolic.[11] They are denounced as serving an international demonic force that threatens Western Christian civilization, a civilization that in reality has very little that is Christian about it.

Thus they discover throug praxis that their innocent period was not in the least impartial. But at this point many are afraid; they lose the courage to face the existential risk of historical commitment. They return to their idealistic illusions, but now as members of the shrewd camp.

They need to be able to justify their return. Hence they claim that the masses, who are "uneducated and incapable," must be protected from losing their faith in God, which is "so beautiful, so sweet, and so edifying"; they must be protected from the "subversive evil of the false Christians who praise the Chinese Cultural Revolution and admire the Cuban Revolution." They sign up for the defense of the faith when what they are really defending is their own class interests, to which that faith is subordinated.

They must then insist on the "neutrality" of the church, whose fundamental task, they say, is to reconcile the irreconcilable through maximum social stability. Thus they castrate the prophetic dimension of the church, whose witness becomes one of fear—fear of change, fear that an unjust world will be radically transformed, fear of getting lost in an uncertain future. But a church that refuses historical involvement is nevertheless involved in history. In fact, those who preach that the church is outside history contradict themselves in practice, because they automatically place themselves at the side of those who refuse to allow the oppressed classes to be. Afraid of this uncertainty, and anxious to avoid the risk of a future that must always be constructed and not just received, the church badly loses its way. It can no longer test itself, either through the denunciation of the unjust world, or the annunciation of a more just world to be built by the historical-social praxis of the oppressed. In this situation, the church can be no more utopian, prophetic, or filled with hope than are the ruling classes to which it is allied.[12] Deprived of its prophetic vision, it takes the road of formalism in bureaucratic rites where hope, detached from the future, becomes only an alienated and alienating abstraction. Instead of stimulating the pilgrim, it invites him to stand still. Basically, it is a church that forbids itself the Easter it preaches. It is a church that is freezing to death, unable to respond to the aspirations of a troubled, utopian and biophile youth to whom one can no longer speak a medieval language, and who are not interested in discussing the sex of angels, for these youths are challenged by the drama of their own history. Most of these young people are well aware that the basic problem of Latin America is not the laziness of the people, or their inferiority, or their lack of education. The problem is imperialism. And they know that this imperialism is neither abstraction nor slogan but tangible reality, an invading, destroying presence. Until this basic contradiction is overcome, Latin America and the rest of the Third World cannot develop. It can only modernize.[13] For without liberation, there can be no real development of dependent societies.

A Theology of Liberation

Many theologians who are today becoming more and more historically involved with the oppressed rightly speak of a political theology of liberation rather than one of modernizing development. These theologians can begin to speak to the troubling questions of a generation that chooses revolutionary change rather than the reconciliation of irreconcilables. They know very well that only the oppressed, as the social class that has been forbidden to speak, can become the utopians, the prophets, and the messengers of hope, provided that their future is not simply a reformed repetition of the present. Their future is the realization of their liberation—without which they cannot be.[14] Only they can denounce the order that crushes them, transforming that order in praxis; only they can announce a new world, one that is constantly being recreated and renewed.

That is why their hope rests not in an invitation to halt the pilgrimage, an invitation offered not only by the traditionalists but also by the alienating modernizers. Their hope lies in the call "Forward, march!", not the senseless wandering of those who give up and run, but the "Forward, march" of those who hold history in their hands, who create it and re-create themselves in it. It is the "Forward, march" they will eventually have to embark upon if they are to experience death as an oppressed class and be born again to liberation.

We must stress yet again that this journey cannot be made within their consciousness. It must be made in history. No one can make such a journey simply in the inside of his being.

But there are a growing number of people who, whether or not they still claim to be Christians, commit themselves to the liberation of the dominated classes. Their experience teaches them that being Christian doesn't necessarily imply being reactionary, just as being revolutionary doesn't always imply being demonic. Being revolutionary implies struggling against oppression and exploitation, for the liberation and freedom of the oppressed, concretely and not idealistically.[15] In their new apprenticeship they finally realize that it is not sufficient to give lip service to the idea that men and women are human beings if nothing is done objectively to help them experience what it means to be *persons*. They learn that it is not through good works (Niebuhr's phrase here was "humanitarian") that the oppressed become incarnate as persons. They have, then, managed to overcome the first obstacles that were too much for some of their traveling companions; but that is no guarantee that they will survive the harder trials that lie ahead.

At some point in the process the oppressor's violence will be directed exclusively against the working class, usually sparing committed intellectuals, since in the last analysis they belong to the same group as the ruling class; at other times, however, their violence will be indiscriminate. When this happens, many will retreat, keep quiet, or adjust to the situation; others will react by undertaking new commitments. A basic difference between those who leave and those who stay is that the latter accept, as an integral part of existence, the dramatic tension between past and future, death and life, staying and going, creating and not creating, between saying the word and mutilating silence, between hope and despair, being and nonbeing. It is an illusion to think that human beings can escape this dramatic tension. We have no right so to submerge ourselves in the drama of our own life that we lose ourselves in daily triviality.[16] In fact, if I lose myself in the details of daily life, I lose, at the same time, a vision of the dramatic meaning of my existence. I become either fatalistic or cynical. In the same way, if I try to escape from the daily demands and details to take up my life's dramatic character—but without at the same time becoming historically involved—I can have no other destiny than to fall into an empty intellectualism, equally alienating. I shall then see existence as something impossible and hopeless. I have no other chance of conquering the alienating trivialities of daily life than by way of historical praxis, which is social and not individual. It is only insofar as I accept to the full my responsibility within the play of this dramatic tension that I make myself a conscious presence in the world.

I cannot permit myself to be a mere spectator. On the contrary, I must demand my place in the process of change. So the dramatic tension between the past and the future, death and life, being and nonbeing, is no longer a kind of dead end for me; I can see it for what it really is: a permanent challenge to which I must respond. And my response can be none other than my historical praxis—in other words, revolutionary praxis.

The revolution does not do away with the dramatic tension of our existence. It resolves the antagonistic contradictions that make that tension even more dramatic, but precisely because it participates in that tension it is as permanent as the tension itself.

A reign of undisturbed peace is unthinkable in history. History is *becoming;* it is a human event. But rather than feeling disappointed and frightened by critical discovery of the tension in which my humanity places me, I discover in that tension the joy of being.

At the same time, dramatic tension cannot be reduced to my own existential experience. I cannot of course deny the singularity and uniqueness of my existence but that does not make my existence, in itself, isolated from other existences, a model of absolute meaning. On the contrary, it is in the intersubjectivity, mediated by objectivity, that my existence makes sense. "I exist" does not come before "we exist," but is fulfilled in it. The individualistic, bourgeois concept of existence cannot grasp the true social and historical basis of human existence. It is of the essence of humanity that men and women create their own existence, in a creative act that is always social and historical even while having its specific, personal dimensions.

Existence is not despair, but risk. If I don't exist dangerously, I cannot be. But if my existence is historical, the existential risk is not a simple abstract category; it is also historical. That means that to exist is first and foremost to risk oneself, though the form and effectiveness of the risk will vary from person to person and from place to place. I do not assume risk in Brazil as a Swiss assumes it in Geneva, even if we are both of one political mind. Our sociohistorical reality will condition the form our risk will take. To seek to universalize the form and content of existential risk is an idealistic illusion, unacceptable to anyone who thinks dialectically.

Dialectical thinking constitutes one of the major challenges to those who follow the option we are talking about here. It is not always easy, even for those who identify with the people, to overcome a petit-bourgeois education that is individualistic and intellectual, dichotomizing theory and practice, the transcendent and the mundane, intellectual work and manual work.[17] This trademark shows constantly in attitudes and behavior patterns in which the dominated classes become mere objects of their "impatient revolutionism."

The Role of the Church

In trying, now, to analyze more deeply the role of the church, especially its educational role, we must return to some of the points made above, first of all, to the fact that it cannot be politically neutral. It cannot avoid making a choice, and therefore we in turn cannot discuss the church's role abstractly or metaphysically. Its choice will condition its whole approach to education—its concept, objectives, methods, processes, and all its auxiliary effects. This conditioning affects the theological training of the leadership of the militant church, as well as the education dispensed by the church. Even theological education and reflection are touched.

In a class society, the power elite necessarily determines what education will be, and therefore its objectives. The objectives will certainly not be opposed to the elite's interests. As we have already said, it would be supremely naive to imagine that the elite would in any way promote or accept an education that stimulated the oppressed to discover the *raison d'être* of the social structure. The most that could be expected is that the elite might permit talk of such education, and occasional experiments that could be immediately suppressed should the status quo be threatened.

Thus the Episcopal Conference of Latin America (CELAM) can talk about liberating education in nearly all its official documents; as long as it is not put into practice, nothing serious will happen to it. At any rate, we should not be surprised (though this is not based on any hard evidence) if one day CELAM is severely restricted by the power elite, through the antiprophetic church of which we spoke. This church, which is freezing to death in the warm bosom of the bourgeoisie, can certainly not tolerate any ideas, even if only verbal, that the elite considers diabolic.

Our task in considering the role of the church in education would be simplified if we could count on coherence between church and gospel. In that case, it would be sufficient to look at the dependent condition of Latin American society (with the exception of Cuba and up to a point Nicaragua) and set up a strategy of action for the church. The reality, however, is different. We cannot think in a vacuum.

It is not possible to speak objectively of the educational role of the various denominations as being unified and coherent. On the contrary, their roles differ, sometimes opposing each other, according to the political line, whether evident, hidden, or disguised, which the different churches are living out in history. The traditionalist church, first of all, is still intensely colonialist. It is a missionary church, in the worst sense of the word—a necrophiliac winner of souls; hence its taste for masochistic emphasis on sin, hellfire, and eternal damnation. The mundane, dichotomized from the transcendental, is the "filth" in which humans have to pay for their sins. The more they suffer, the more they purify themselves, finally reaching heaven and eternal rest. Work is not, for them, the action of men and women on the world, transforming and re-creating, but rather the price that must be paid for being human.

In this traditionalist line, whether it be Protestant or Catholic, we find what the Swiss sociologist Christian Lalive calls the haven of the masses.[18] This view of the world, of life, satisfies the fatalistic and frightened consciousness of the oppressed at a certain moment of their historical experience. They find in it a kind of healing for their existential fatigue. So it is that the more the masses are drowned in their culture of silence, with all the violence that this implies on the part of the oppressors, the more the masses tend to take refuge in churches that offer that sort of ministry.[19] Submerged in this culture of silence, where the only voice to be heard is that of the ruling classes, they see this church as a sort of womb in which they can hide from an aggressive society. In despising this world as a world of sin, vice, and impurity, they are in one sense taking their revenge on their oppressors, its owners. It is as if they were saying to the bosses, "You are powerful—but the world over which your power holds sway is an evil one and we reject it." Forbidden as a subordinate social class to have their say, they fool themselves that the prayers for salvation they voice in their haven are a genuine form of speaking out.

None of this resolves the real problems of the oppressed. Their catharsis actually alienates them further, for it directs their anger against the world and not against the social system that is ruining the world. Thus, seeing the world itself as the antagonist, they attempt the impossible: to renounce the world's mediation in their pilgrimage. By doing so, they hope to reach transcendence without passing by way of the mundane; they want metahistory without experiencing history; they want salvation without knowing liberation. The pain of domination leads them to accept this historical anaesthesia in the hope that it will strengthen them to fight sin and the devil—leaving untouched all the while the real causes of their oppression. They cannot see, beyond their present situation, the untested feasibility, the future as a liberation project that they must create for themselves.

This traditional type of church is usually found in backward, closed societies, mostly agricultural, which depend upon the export of raw materials and have only a minimal internal market; here the culture of silence is fundamental. Like the archaic social structures, the traditionalist church remains unchanged throughout the modernization of these societies. The force of such traditionalist religion is seen even in the urban centers being transformed under the impact of industrialization.[20] Only a qualitative change in the consciousness of the people can overcome the need to see the church as the haven of the masses. And as we have seen, this qualitative change does not happen automatically, mechanically, or merely within consciousness.

Furthermore, technological modernization does not necessarily make people more capable of critical analysis, because it too is not neutral. It is dependent on the ideology that commands it.

For all these reasons and for many more that would take too long to analyze, the traditionalist line is unquestionably allied to the ruling classes, whether or not it is aware of this. The role that these churches can (and do) play in the field of education is conditioned then by their view of the world, of religion, and of human beings and their destiny. Their idea of education and its application cannot help being paralyzing, alienating, and alienated. Only those who hold this perspective critically—rather than naively—will be able to escape from their trap through praxis, by entering into a totally different commitment to the dominated classes and so becoming truly prophetic.

The Modernizing Church

Some churches abandon the traditionalist perspective for a new attitude. History shows that the new position begins to emerge when modernizing elements replace the traditional structures of society. The masses of the people, previously almost completely submerged in the historical process, now begin to emerge in response to industrialization.[21] Society also changes. New challenges are presented to the dominating classes, demanding different answers.

The imperialist interests that condition this transition become more and more aggressive. They use various means of penetration into and control over the dependent society. At a given moment the emphasis on industrialization gives rise to a nationalist ideology of development that makes a case for, among other things, a pact between the national bourgeoisie and the emerging proletariat.

Economists have been the first to analyze this process, followed closely by sociologists and some educators. Together they plan and put into practice the concept of social planning. At this point, the Economic Commission for Latin America (CEPAL) begins to play a decisive role, both through technical missions and through its adherence to development politics. Later comes the contribution of the Latin American Institute for Economic and Social Planning (ILPES), an organ of the United Nations whose job is to educate economists for the entire South American continent.

Obviously, none of this happens by chance or in isolation. The process is an intrinsic part of the history that Latin American societies are living, in varying degrees of intensity. This complex movement, like the different perspectives produced in response to the so-called backwardness of Latin America, is neither accidental nor the result of some caprice.

As we have seen, imperialistic economic interests, such as the need for wider markets, force the national elite (which is almost always a purely local expression of a foreign elite) to find ways to reform the archaic structures without, at the same time, frustrating their interests. For imperialism and its national allies, the important thing is that this reformist process—publicly called development—should not affect the basic relationship between the master society and its dependent societies. Development is acceptable, but it must not alter the state of dependence! With the exception of a few minor points that will not alter the state of the subordinate society, the political, economic, and cultural decisions concerning the transformation of the dependent society will be made in the master society.

So it is that the Latin American societies, with the exception of Cuba since its revolution, and up to a point Nicaragua, are modernizing rather than developing in the real sense of the word. Latin America can only truly develop when the fundamental contradiction of dependence is resolved. This demands that decision-making on change must rest in the hands of the masses of oppressed people in the society concerned; it must be independent from a superimposed bourgeois elite.

Thus development is liberation on two levels: the whole dependent society liberating itself from imperialism, and the oppressed social classes liberating themselves from the oppressive elite. This is because real development is impossible in a class society.

The process of imperialist expansion produces new political and social situations. The process of transition in the dependent society implies the contradictory presences of both a proletariat that is being modernized and a traditional proletariat, a technico-professional petite bourgeoisie and a traditional middle class, a traditional church and a modernizing church, a highly baroque academic education and the technico-professional education demanded by industrialization.[22]

So it is that in spite of what the mechanists think, the movement from one stage to another is not automatic. There are no rigid geographical frontiers between the stages; both dimensions coexist in transition.

The proletariat of the modernization phase lives in a new historical experience, that of transition, giving birth to a new political action style: populism. Its directors play the game of mediator between the emerging common people and the ruling classes.[23] Populism is unthinkable in a situation where the common people have not yet made their emergence. It is found in urban centers rather than in the latifundia or estates where the peasant masses are still submerged.

At the same time, in the historical framework that gives birth to it, populism tends toward do-goodism; hence its possibilities of manipulation. The emerging masses of common people are intensely conditioned by their experience in the culture of silence.[24]

During the process of emergence they obviously have no class consciousness, since their former state of immersion gave them no chance to develop it. They are, then, as ambiguous as the populism that attempts to respond to them. On the one hand they make demands. On the other, they accept the formulas of do-goodism and manipulation. That is why the traditionalist churches also survive during the period of transition, even in the modernized urban centers. These churches often choose to enhance their own prestige, since after the stage of populism there may well be a new phase characterized by violent military regimes. Repression, reactivating the old life styles of the masses (the culture of silence), forces them to take refuge in the church. As we have seen, these churches, existing side by side with those that have modernized, modernize too in certain respects, thereby becoming more efficient in their traditionalism.

We have seen that the modernization process of the dependent society never gets translated into fundamental changes in the relationship between the dependent society and the master society, and that the emergence of the masses does not by itself constitute their critical consciousness. In the same way, it is interesting to note, the churches' pilgrimage toward modernization never gets translated into historic involvement with the oppressed people in any real sense that leads toward that people's liberation.

Challenged by the increased efficiency of a society that is modernizing its archaic structures, the modernizing church improves its bureaucracy so that it can be more efficient in its social activities (its do-goodism) and in its pastoral activities. It replaces empirical means by technical processes. Its former charity centers directed by lay persons (in the Catholic church by the Daughters of Mary) become known as community centers directed by social workers. And the men and women who were previously known by their own names are today numbers in a card index.

Mass media (which are actually media for issuing communiqués to the masses) become an irresistible attraction to the churches. But the modern and modernizing church can hardly be condemned for attempting to perfect its working tools; what is more serious is the political option that clearly conditions the process of modernization. Like the traditionalist churches, of which they are a new version, they are not committed to the oppressed but to the power elite. That is why they defend structural reform over the radical transformation of structures; they speak of the humanization of capitalism rather than its total suppression.

The traditionalist churches alienate the oppressed social classes by encouraging them to view the world as evil. The modernizing churches alienate them in a different way: by defending the reforms that maintain the status quo. By reducing such expressions as *humanism* and *humanization* to abstract categories, the modern churches empty them of any real meaning. Such phrases become mere slogans whose only contribution is to serve the reactionary forces. In truth, there is no humanization without liberation, just as there is no liberation without a revolutionary transformation of the class society, for in the class society all humanization is impossible. Liberation becomes concrete only when society is changed, not when its structures are simply modernized.

Insofar as the modernizing churches busy themselves with no more than peripheral changes and plead the case of neocapitalistic measures, they will have their audience only among the naive or the shrewd. The young people who are neither naive nor shrewd but are challenged by the drama of Latin America or other parts of the Third World cannot accept the invitation of the modernizing churches that support conservative and reformist positions. Not only do they refuse the invitation, it provokes them into assuming attitudes that are not always valid, such as the objectivist position discussed elsewhere in this article.

The churches' conservative position, rejected by these young people, does not contradict their modernism, for the modernization of which we are talking is eminently conservative, since it reforms in order to preserve the status quo. Hence the churches give the impression of moving while actually they are standing still. They create the illusion of marching on while really stabilizing themselves. They die because they refuse to die.

This is the kind of church that would still say to Christ today, "Why leave, Master, if everything here is so beautiful, so good?" Their language conceals rather than reveals. It speaks of the poor or of the underprivileged rather than the oppressed. While it sees the alienations of the ruling class and dominated class on the same level, it ignores the antagonism between them, the result of the system that created them. But if the system alienates both groups, it alienates each in a different way. The rulers are alienated to the degree that, sacrificing their *being* for a false "*having*," they are drugged with power and so stop *being*; the dominated, prevented to a certain degree from "*having*," finish with so little power that *being* is impossible. Turning work into merchandise, the system creates those who buy it and those who sell it. The error of the naive and the shrewdness of the shrewd is seen in their affirmation that such a contradiction is a purely moral question.

The ruling classes, as is the logic of the class system, prohibit the dominated class from *being*. In this process the ruling class itself ceases to *be*. The system itself keeps them from rising above the contradiction, from any movement that would end their alienation as well as that of those they dominate. The dominated alone are called to fulfill this task in history. The ruling class, as such, cannot carry it out. What they can do—within their historical limits—is to reform and to modernize the system according to the new demands the system allows them to perceive, thus in effect maintaining that which results in the alienation of all.

Under the conditions in which the modernizing churches act, their concepts of education, its objectives, its application, all must form a coherent unity within their general political position. That is why, even though they speak of liberating education, they are conditioned by their vision of liberation as an individual activity that should take place through a change of consciousness and not through the social and historical praxis of human beings. So they end up by putting the accent on methods that can be considered neutral. Liberating education for the modernizing church is finally reduced to liberating the students from blackboards, static classes, and textbook curricula, and offering them projectors and other audio-visual accessories, more dynamic classes, and a new technico-professional teaching.

The Prophetic Church

Finally, another kind of church has been taking shape in the Third World though it is not often visible as a coherent totality. It is a church as old as Christianity itself, without being traditional; as new as Christianity, without being modernizing. It is the prophetic church. Opposed and attacked by both traditionalist and modernizing churches, as well as by the elite of the power structures, this utopian, prophetic, and hope-filled movement rejects do-goodism and palliative reforms in order to commit itself to the dominated social classes and to radical social change.

In contrast with the churches considered above, it rejects all static forms of thought. It accepts becoming, in order to *be*. Because it thinks critically this prophetic church cannot think of itself as neutral. Nor does it try to hide its choice. Therefore it does not separate worldliness from transcendence or salvation from liberation. It knows that what finally counts is not the "I am" or the "I know," the "I free myself" or the "I save myself;" nor even the "I teach you," "I free you," or "I save you," but the "we are," "we know," "we save ourselves."

This prophetic line can only be understood as an expression of the dramatic and challenging situation of the Third World. It emerges when the contradictions in society become apparent. It is at this moment, too, that revolution is seen as the means of liberation for the oppressed people, and the military coup as the reactionary countermove.

The world's prophetic Christians may disagree among themselves, especially at the point of action, but they are the ones who have renounced their innocence in order to join the oppressed classes, and who remain faithful to their commitment. Protestant or Catholic—from the point of view of this prophetic position the division is of no importance—clergy or lay, they have all had to travel a hard route of experience from their idealistic visions toward a dialectical vision of reality. They have learned, not only as a result of their praxis with the people, but also from the courageous example of many young people. They now see that reality, a process and not a static fact, is full of contradictions, and that social conflicts are not metaphysical categories but rather historical expressions of the confrontation of these contradictions. Any attempt, therefore, to solve conflict without touching the contradictions that have generated it only stifles the conflict and at the same time strengthens the ruling class.

The prophetic position demands a critical analysis of the social structures in which the conflict takes place. This means that it demands of its followers a knowledge of sociopolitical science, since this science cannot be neutral; this demands an ideological choice.

Such prophetic perspective does not represent an escape into a world of unattainable dreams. It demands a scientific knowledge of the world as it really is. For to denounce the present reality and announce its radical transformation into another reality capable of giving birth to new men and women implies gaining through praxis a new knowledge of reality. The dominated classes must take part in this denunciation and annunciation. It cannot be done if they are left out of the picture. The prophetic position is not petit-bourgeois. It is well aware that authentic action demands a permanent process that only reaches its maximal point when the dominated class, through praxis, also becomes prophetic, utopian and full of hope—in other words, revolutionary. A society in a state of permanent revolution cannot manage without a permanent prophetic vision. Without it, society stagnates and is no longer revolutionary.[25]

In the same way, no church can be really prophetic if it remains the haven of the masses or the agent of modernization and conservation. The prophetic church is no home for the oppressed, alienating them further by empty denunciations. On the contrary, it invites them to a new Exodus. Nor is the prophetic church one that chooses modernization and thereby does no more than stagnate. Christ was no conservative. The prophetic church, like him, must move forward constantly, forever dying and forever being reborn. In order to be, it must always be in a state of *becoming*. The prophetic church must also accept an existence that is in dramatic tension between past and future, staying and going, speaking the word and keeping silence, being and not being. There is no prophecy without risk.

This prophetic attitude, which emerges in the praxis of numerous Christians in the challenging historical situation of Latin America, is accompanied by a rich and very necessary theological reflection. The theology of so-called development gives way to the theology of liberation—a prophetic, utopian theology, full of hope. Little does it matter that this theology is not yet well systematized. Its content arises from the hopeless situation of dependent, exploited, invaded societies. It is stimulated by the need to rise above the contradictions that explain and produce that dependence. Since it is prophetic, this theology of liberation cannot attempt to reconcile the irreconcilable.

At this moment in history, theology cannot spend its time discussing secularization (which in the end is the modern form of sacralization)[26] or try to entertain us with the death of God discussion, which in many ways reveals an acritical tendency of complete adaptation by the "uni-dimensionalized and depoliticized man of the affluent societies," as Hugo Assmann has aptly phrased it.[27]

To digress a moment from our specific subject, we should add here that this prophetic attitude toward the world and history is by no means exclusive to Latin America or other areas of the Third World. It is not an exotic attitude peculiar to underdevelopment—first because the original Christian position is itself prophetic, at whatever point in time and place. Only the particular content of its witness will vary, according to the precise historical circumstances. Moreover, the concept of the Third World is ideological and political, not geographic. The so-called First World has within it and against it its own Third World. And the Third World has its First World, represented by the ideology of domination and the power of the ruling classes. The Third World is in the last analysis the world of silence, of oppression, of dependence, of exploitation, of the violence exercised by the ruling classes on the oppressed.

Europeans and North Americans, with their technological societies, have no need to go to the Third World countries in order to become prophetic. They need only go to the outskirts of their big cities, without naiveté or shrewdness, and there they will find sufficient stimulus to do some fresh thinking for themselves. They will find themselves confronted with various expressions of the Third World. They can begin to understand the concern that gives rise to the prophetic position in Latin America.

Thus it is clear that the educational role of the prophetic church must be totally different from that of the other churches we have discussed. Education must be an instrument of transforming action, a political praxis at the service of permanent human liberation. This, let us repeat, does not happen only in the consciousness of people, but presupposes a radical change of structures, in which process consciousness will itself be transformed.

From the prophetic point of view, it makes little difference in what specific area education happens; it will always be an effort to clarify the concrete context in which the teacher-students and student-teachers are educated and are united by their presence in action. It will always be a demythologizing praxis.

This brings us back to our opening statement: the church, education, and the role of the churches in education can only be discussed historically. It is in history that mankind is called to respond to the prophetic movement in the Third World.

NOTES

1. *This chapter first appeared in *Study Encounter*, vol. 9, no. 1 (1973). It was translated by William Bloom with the help of Esther Meyer, Helen Mackintosh, and Helen Franco.

2. Reinhold Niebuhr, *Moral Man and Immoral Society* (New York: Charles Scribner's Sons, 1960).

3. A phrase I owe to Erich Fromm, *The Heart of Man* (London: Routledge and Kegan Paul, 1965).

4. Referring to the moralists, Niebuhr says: "They do not recognize that when collective power, whether in the form of imperialism or class domination, exploits weakness, it can never be dislodged unless power is raised against it. . . . Modern religious idealists usually follow in the wake of social scientists in advocating compromise and accommodation as the way to social justice." Fromm, *The Heart of Man*, pp. xii and xix.

5. "For the purposes of the historian, i.e. the student of micro-history, or of history 'as it happened' (and of the present 'as it happens') as distinct from the general and rather abstract models of the historical transformation of societies, class and the problem of class consciousness are inseparable. Class in the full sense only comes into existence at the historical moment when classes begin to acquire consciousness of themselves as such." E.J. Hobsbawm "Class Consciousness in History," in Istvan Mesaros, (ed.), *Aspects of History and Class Consciousness* (London: Routledge and Kegan Paul, 19--), p. 6.

6. On this, see Georg Lukács, *Histoire et Conscience de Classe* (Paris: Les Editions de Minuit, 1960).

7. Paulo Freire, "Cultural Action: An Introduction," in *Conscientization for Liberation* (Washington, D.C.: CICOP, 1971).

8. See Paulo Freire, *Pedagogy of the Oppressed* (New York: Seabury Press, 1970).

9. A representative of a Latin American elite, answering a journalist's question during an interview, said, "I could never permit an educational process which would awaken the potential of the masses and put me in the difficult situation of having to listen to them. It would be like asking for a rope to hang myself by."

10. Concerning free employment as a necessary condition for human liberty, see *Fifteen Bishops Speak for the Third World* (Mexico: CIDOC, 1967). pp.1–11.

11. Dom Heider Câmara, the prophetic archbishop of Olinda and Recife (Brazil), is today considered one of these terrible demons. It's always the same. The necrophiles can never stand the presence of a biophile.

12. From the beginning of modern times, hopes for something new from God have emigrated from the Church and have been invested in revolution and rapid social change. It was most often reaction and conservatism that remained in the Church. Thus the Christian Church became "religious". "That is, she cultivated and apotheosized tradition. Her authority was sanctioned by what had been in force always and everywhere from the earliest times." Jürgen Moltmann, *Religion, Revolution and the Future* (New York: Charles Scribner's Sons, 1969). pp. 5–6.

13. This theme is more fully developed in my *Pedagogy of the Oppressed*.

14. In reality, only the oppressed can conceive a future that is radically different from their present insofar as they gain a dominated class consciousness. The oppressors, as the ruling class, can only imagine the future as the preservation of their present—their role of oppressors. So while the future of the first rests in the revolutionary transformation of society—a condition for

their own liberation—the future of the second presupposes mere social modernization in which they can maintain their position as rulers.

15. At this point, of course, no revolutionary, Christian or non-Christian, can accept a church that innocently or shrewdly aligns itself with the ruling class, loses its utopian dimension, and empties itself of prophetic mission. There is no need to denounce such a church. It denounces itself through its defense, surreptitious or not, of the ruling class.

16. Karel Kosik, *Dialéctica de lo concreto* (Mexico: Grijalbo, 1967).

17. The term *mundane* here refers to the condition of incarnation in the world.

18. See his *Haven of the Masses: A Study of the Pentacostal Movement in Chile* (London: Lutterworth Press, 1969).

19. A sociological analysis of this fact in Latin America is essential, but it is important that the starting point of such research be social class structures and not the religious phenomenon itself.

20. See Beatriz Muniz de Souza, *A Experiência da salvação: pentecostais em São Paulo* (São Paulo: Duas Cidades, 1969).

21. Paulo Freire, *La Educación como práctica de la libertad* (Montevideo: Tierra Nueva, 19--). Also in French: *La Pratique de la liberté* (Paris: Eds. du Cerf, 19--).

22. See Fernando Henrique Cardoso, *Politique et développement dans les sociétés dépendantes* (Paris, Editions Anthropos, 1971).

23. See Francisco Weffort, *Classes populares e política (Contribução ao estudo do populismo)* (Universidade São Paulo, 1968).

24. Paulo Freire, *Cultural Action for Freedom* (London: Penguin, 1972).

25. A prophetic vision need not be the result of a religious position.

26. There are no societies more "sacral" than those that are bourgeois. They react viciously to the slightest attempt to disrupt patterns they consider universal, eternal, and perfect.

27. *Opresión-Liberación: Desafio a los Cristianos* (Montevideo: Tierra Nueva, 1971).

CHAPTER ELEVEN

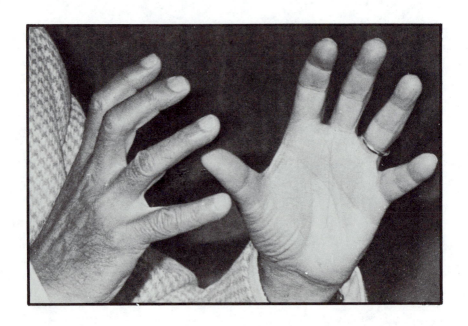

In Praise of *A Black Theology of Liberation* by James Cone

There is a category of book that so challenges and fascinates us that we can't put it down until, along with the author, we reach the very last word. *A Black Theology of Liberation* is one of those books.

In 1970 when *A Black Theology of Liberation* had just been published in the United States, I received a copy while in Geneva from a young friend in New York, one of Cone's students who had regularly taken part in a seminar I had coordinated in 1969 at Harvard University. Cone was not unknown to me. I had read his first book and even though it lacked the formal qualities he later developed in his second book, it clearly distinguished him. That was the feeling I had in 1969 when I finished reading *Black Theology and Black Power* in Cambridge, Massachusetts.

This book, I said to myself, promises something more rigorous to come.

I received *A Black Theology of Liberation*, then, with ready expectations. Cone's clarity, his seriousness of analysis, and his commitment to the oppressed have not surprised me. All of this is actually confirmation of what I've already stated.

I remember perfectly that I received my copy the day before a trip to Rome, where I was to coordinate a week-long seminar on education for liberation. At home that night after dinner, I accepted the book's invitation and I began my intimate relationship with it. I gave it a careful reading and I was spellbound page after page, not putting it down until the early morning and finishing it for the first time some hours later, en route from Geneva to Rome. When I returned to Geneva, I read it for a second time and then wrote to Cone, expressing my impressions and the importance of its immediate publication in Latin America, since black theology (for which Cone is the foremost proponent in the United States) is unquestionably linked with the theology of liberation flourishing today in Latin America.

The prophetic nature of both these theologies lies not in their merely speaking for those who are forbidden to speak, but, most important, in their side-by-side struggle with those silenced so that they can effectively speak the word by revolutionarily transforming the society that reduces them to silence. "To say the word," then, is not just to utter "good morning" or to follow the prescriptions of the powerful who command and exploit. "To say the word" is to make history that can be made and remade. The dominated and silenced classes can only say the word when they take history into their own hands and dismantle the oppressive system that crushes them. Through revolutionary praxis, along with a critical and vigilant leadership, the dominated classes learn to "proclaim" their world, thus discovering the real reasons for their past silence. Hence, the eminently political nature of black theology in the United States and the theology of liberation in Latin America.

Both these theologies tend increasingly to sanction political action, but this doesn't mean that they are aberrations from a theological "purity" or a hypothetical neutral theology.

To use our expression, which Cone admires, a white theology is just as political as a black theology or a theology for liberation in Latin America. Although it's easily seen through, politics hides the orientation of a white theology toward defending dominant class interests. This is why, though simulating neutrality, white theology is preoccupied with the conciliation of things that cannot be conciliated, why it negates so insistently the differences among social classes and their struggle, and why in its incursions for social good it doesn't go beyond the kind of modernizing reformisms that preserve the structures of domination.

Thinking from the viewpoint of the dominant classes, theologians of this impossible neutrality employ mystifying language. They consistently attempt to soften the harsh, oppressive real world and exhort the dominated classes (invariably labeled as poor or less fortunate) to face their sacrifice with resignation. The pain and degrading discrimination they suffer—their very existence as a form of death in life—should be taken by the dominated classes as a means of purification for their sins. In short, the oppressed should thank "the rich" for the opportunities they offer them to save themselves.

The dominated classes need to transform the suffering arising from their imposed struggle, not merely submit to it. Whereas submission to suffering amounts to a form of annihilation, transformation of suffering becomes a faith that moves it. Only that faith which is born today, and in the "today" of the struggle, can give meaning to the future, not as an alienating vagueness or as a predetermined entity, but as a task of construction, a "deed of liberty."

Those who promote a white theology propose an even greater passivity for the oppressed classes by disregarding the unity between reconciliation and liberation. For them, reconciliation is nothing more than the dominated acceding to the will of the dominant. All this supposes it were possible to reduce reconciliation to a kind of pact between dominant and dominated, "rich" and "poor": a pact that accepts the continuation of the oppressed reality in which the dominated, in return, receive efficient and modernized social assistance.

Such an elitist concept of reconciliation will find no acceptance in the theology of liberation in Latin America or in the black theology of liberation for which, again, James Cone is one of the most eloquent representatives. In truth, any reconciliation between oppressors and oppressed, as social classes, presupposes the liberation of the oppressed, forged by themselves through their own revolutionary praxis.

The important point right now, though, is that the reader begin a convivial relationship with the thinking of James Cone. So to conclude this brief introduction I'll only add that in emerging from an incredible reality, a "diabolic" real world of racism in the United States, his thinking gains a singular force. In his theological reflections on this reality, he doesn't present black people as though from another world, typecast as curious foreigners. James Cone is a committed man, "saturated" in this real world, which he analyzes with the authority of one who has experienced it.

A *Black Theology of Liberation* is for this reason a passionate book, passionately written. In reading it, some will be chilled from anger, others will tremble with fear. Many readers, though, will find a stimulus here for their own struggles. James Cone does not attempt any more than this.

CHAPTER TWELVE

A Conversation with Paulo Freire

DAC:* In spite of the increasing acceptance of your thought in the United States, Europe, and Latin America, we find the most severe criticisms of your work in Latin America, the beginning point of your theory and practice.[1] These criticisms rest on two points: first, you are accused of having lost contact with the Latin American reality; second, you are accused of idealism and reformism. What do you say in response to these criticisms?

Freire: Let me say to begin with, and I want to underline the fact, that I am in the habit of taking seriously criticisms directed against me. Confronted with criticism I do not assume the air of someone attacked or injured. Nevertheless, sometimes there are among the criticisms those

*The Institute of Cultural Action (see n. 1 end of chapter).

that, by their very fragility, do not deserve serious attention. I do not see, for example, why I should worry about the charge that I have put aside my concerned involvement with Latin America when I accepted the post of visiting professor at Harvard. On the other hand, I'm profoundly interested in criticism aimed at the content of my pedagogical and political thought that interprets me as idealist, subjectivist, or reformist. It seems to me, however, that those who thus classify me by drawing on certain naive phrases that can be lifted out of my works—and are today the object of my own self-criticism—must try to accompany me through the steps of my own evolution. In effect, I don't hold any simple or immodest illusions about reaching a state of absolute critical ability. It seems to me that the important thing is to see which of the two aspects—the naive or the critical—is imposing itself as my praxis and reflection gradually develop.

IDAC: Nevertheless, it seems to us that the accusation of idealism rests on a real base if one considers the historic experience of the program for the "conscientization" of the masses that took place in Brazil in 1962 to 1964. At that time the extremely rapid politicization of people obtained through a literacy program did not suffice for the building of a base of resistance to the military *coup d'état,* which swept away the hopes that had been born among peasants and unskilled urban workers who had experienced conscientization. If we agree that a process of becoming aware in an oppressive situation is not sufficient for changing that reality, then we should have had from the very beginning of the Brazilian experience the development of a political organization of the masses of people with a strategy capable of orienting their action toward a social and political transformation.

Freire: Actually, one of the weakest points of my work, on which I've done an autocritique, is the process of conscientization. To the degree that, especially in my first theoretical works, I made no—or almost no—reference to the political character of education and I neglected the problem of social classes and their struggle, I opened the door to every sort of reactionary interpretation and practice, leading to many distortions of what conscientization must really be. And how often I've been criticized—not for a lack of clarity in the analysis and the theoretical basis of conscientization—but quite to the contrary many of these criticisms reveal the mechanical objectivist position, antidialectical in itself, of those who express them. Insofar as they are mechanists, denying the very existence of consciousness, they reject, as a consequence, conscientization. I want, then, to restate that while all the time trying to go beyond my ever-present frailties, I see no reason to reject the role of conscientization in the revolutionary process.

IDAC: We agree with you that often these criticisms have been inspired by what you call mechanical and objectivist positions. But Marx insisted that the revolutionary situation implies not only objective factors: the existence of an oppressive reality imposed on classes or social groups, who become the living negation of this system of exploitation. It also implies, he insists, subjective factors: the consciousness of this oppressive reality on the part of the exploited classes and their readiness to act for the overthrow of the established order. These past few years have been marked by two different treatments of the subjective pole. Either there was a kind of eclipse of it in the dialectical relationship with the belief that revolutionary action only becomes possible after the fulfillment of certain infrastructural conditions, such as the full development of capitalism in the underdeveloped countries as a precondition to the transition toward socialism. We have also seen a sort of perversion of the subjective element: Stalinist willfulness or an overestimation of the capacity of small *avant-garde* action groups cut off from the masses in a kind of *foquismo*. Nevertheless, the historical failure of objectivism and of these two deviations of subjectivism has put the question of the subjective factor, as an agent for the transformation of reality, at the center of the contemporary political debate. How do you see this situation?

Freire: This question brings us to the very heart of a fundamental problem that has always preoccupied philosophy—especially modern philosophy. I refer to the question of the relationship between subject and object, consciousness and reality, thought and being, theory and practice. Any attempt to deal with the relationship that is based on the subject-object dualism, while denying their *dialectical unity,* is unable to satisfactorily explain this relationship. In breaking down the subject-object dialectical unity, the dualist vision implies the negation either of objectivity (submitting it to the powers of a consciousness created at will) or of the reality of the consciousness—a transformed one. In the first hypothesis we have the subjectivist error, the expression of an antidialectical and pre-Hegelian idealism. In the second, we are dealing with the mechanical objectivist one, equally antidialectical.

In reality, consciousness is not just a copy of the real, nor is the real only a capricious construction of consciousness. It is only by way of an understanding of the dialectical unity, in which we find solidarity between subjectivity and objectivity, that we can get away from the subjectivist error as well as the mechanical error. And then we must take into account the role of consciousness or of the conscious being in the transformation of reality.

How can one explain, for example, in subjectivist terms the position of human beings—as individuals, a generation, or a social class—confronted with a given historical situation in which they "fit" independent of either their consciousness or their will? And how to explain, on the other hand, the same problem from a mechanical point of view? If consciousness arbitrarily creates reality, a generation or social class could, in rejecting the given situation in which they live, transform it by a simple relevant gesture. Similarly, if consciousness were only a simple reflection of reality, the given situation would be eternally the given situation. Reality would be the determinant subject in itself. Human beings would be only the yielding objects. In other words, the given situation would change of itself. That means seeing history as a mythical entity outside of and superior to human beings, able to capriciously command them from above and beyond. I think just now of Marx and what he wrote in *The Holy Family:*

> History does nothing, possesses no great riches, liberates not one class from its struggles; what does all that, possesses and struggles, is man himself—real, living man. It is not History which uses man as a tool to reach a goal, as though History were a being apart, for History is nothing but the action of man following his objectives.[2]

Actually, when we are faced with a given situation in which we "fit" without being aware, we are up against a concrete condition that poses a challenge. The given situation, as a problematic situation, implies what I called in my last book, *Pedagogy of the Oppressed,* the untested feasibility, that is, the constructable future.[3] The accomplishment of this untested feasibility, which demands going beyond the point blocked by living without reference to our consciousness, is only verified in *praxis.* That means, and let us emphasize it, that human beings do not get beyond the concrete situation, the condition in which they find themselves, only by their consciousness or their intentions, however good those intentions may be. The possibilities that I had for transcending the narrow limits of a five-by-two-foot cell in which I was locked after the April 1964 Brazilian *coup d'état,* were not sufficient to change my condition as a prisoner. I was always in the cell, deprived of freedom, even if I could imagine the outside world. On the other hand, the praxis is not blind action, deprived of intention or of finality. It is action and reflection. Men and women are human beings because they are historically constituted as beings of praxis, and in the process they have become capable of transforming the world—of giving it meaning.

It is only as beings of praxis, in accepting our concrete situations as a challenging condition, that we are able to change its meaning by our action. That is why a true praxis is impossible in the antidialectical vacuum where we are driven by a subject-object dichotomy. That is why subjectivism and mechanical objectivism are always obstacles to an authentic revolutionary process, no matter what concrete forms they take in praxis. In this sense, subjectivism—throwing itself into a simple verbal denunciation of social injustice, preaching the transformation of consciousness while still leaving intact the structures of society—is just as negative as the willful mechanicalism that, mistrusting a rigorous and permanent scientific analysis of objective reality, becomes equally subjectivist in the measure where it "acts" on invented reality.

It is precisely this mechanical objectivism that discovers idealism or reformism in all references to the role of subjectivity in the revolutionary process. At the heart of the matter these expressions, however different, grow up from the same ideological source: the *petite bourgeoisie*.

Mechanical objectivism is a gross distortion of the Marxist position on the fundamental question of the subject-object relationship. For Marx, these relationships are contradictory and dynamic. Subject and object are not found to be dichotomized or constituting one identity, but one dialectical unity, the same dialectical unity in which we find theory and practice.

IDAC: Do you believe that one can become conscious of a situation of exploitation in what you call the theoretical context, like the circle of culture of the Brazilian experience? In those circles of culture a group of illiterate peasants, at the same time as learning to read a linguistic code, went on to decipher the sociohistorical reality in realizing that their illiteracy was only one aspect of a whole process of economic and social exploitation to which they had been submitted. Or do you think that this becoming conscious, this learning to read and write one's own reality, is only possible *in and by* the action of transforming the oppressive reality?

Freire: The answer to this question requires a few preliminary remarks. First, let's try to see what the theoretical context consists of. Our point of departure is the affirmation that neither subjectivism, on the one hand, nor mechanical objectivism on the other is capable of correctly explaining this problem, which finally is similar to the one of which we just spoke. They are not capable of explaining it correctly because in dichotomizing the subject from the object, they automatically dichotomize the practice from the theory, breaking apart the already mentioned dialectical unity. Cut off from practice, theory becomes a simple verbalism. Separated from theory, practice is nothing but blind activism. That is why there is no authentic praxis outside the dialectical unity, action-reflection, practice-theory. In the same way, there is no *theoretical context* if it is not in a dialectical unity with the *concrete context*. In this context— where the facts are—we find ourselves enveloped by the real but without necessarily comprehending in a critical way why the facts are what they are. In the theoretical context, holding the concrete at arms length, we seek the *raison d'être* of the facts.

In the concrete context, we are subjects and objects in a dialectical relationship with reality. In the theoretical context we play the role of cognitive subjects of the subject-object relationship that occurs in the concrete context, in order to return to the point of better reacting as subjects against reality.

This makes up the unity—not the separation—between practice and theory, action and reflection. But since these moments can really only exist as unity and process, whatever may be the beginning point already demands and also contains the other point. And that is why reflection is only legitimate when it sends us back—as Sartre insists— to the concrete context where it seeks to clarify the facts. In so doing, reflection renders our action more effective over against those facts. In throwing light on an accomplished, action, or one that is being accomplished, authentic reflection clarifies future action, which in its given time will have to be open to renewed reflection.

In the light of all these considerations, it seems clear to me that the illiterate peasants do not need a theoretical context (in our case, the circle of culture) to arrive at an awareness of their objective oppressed situation. This awareness occurs in the concrete context of their life. It is through their daily experience, with all of its dramatic evidence, that they become aware of their oppressed condition. But what their awareness—coming out of an immersion in daily life conditions—does not give them is the *reason* for their exploited condition. This is one of the tasks that we have to accomplish in the theoretical context. Precisely because consciousness is not transformed except in praxis, the theoretical context cannot be reduced to an uninvolved research center. The circle of culture must find ways, which each local reality will indicate, by which it must be transformed into a center for political action. If a radical transformation of social structures, that explains the objective situation in which the peasants are found, does not happen, the peasants continue in the same condition. They continue to be exploited in the same way. It matters little that some among them arrived at an understanding of the reason why their reality is as it is. Actually, the demasking of reality that is not oriented toward clear political action against this same reality simply lacks sense.

Of course, this transforming knowledge is impossible in the framework of the everyday. It is only in the unity of praxis and theory, action and reflection, that we go beyond the alienating character of the everyday, such as our spontaneous way of moving through the world or as a result of actions that are made mechanical or bureaucratic. In these two expressions of daily life, we don't succeed in reaching an irreducible knowledge of facts—facts of which we are hardly aware. From there comes the necessity that we feel to go further than a simple perception of the presence of facts and events, seeking not only their interdependence among them but also the constituting elements of the totality of each, also the necessity of trying to establish a permanent control on our thought processes.

There is, in the last analysis, the dialectical movement (incomprehensible from the subjectivist point of view as well as from the mechanical objectivist perspective) that gets posed as a fundamental demand on every effort of knowing reality. This movement implies, on the one hand, that the subject of an action holds the theoretical tools for dealing with the knowledge of reality and, on the other hand, that the subject recognizes the necessity of readapting them after the results have been attained by their application. By that I mean that the results of the act of knowing must constitute the norms for judging one's own behavior.

IDAC: What you are doing, if we understand correctly, is holding up the political involvement of a scientist, for example, as an essential condition and test for the scientific nature of his knowledge. Or, putting it another way, for you an apolitical science constitutes nothing but a false knowledge. Is that right?

Freire: Yes. Every student worthy of the name knows very well that the so-called neutrality of science (from which flows the equally famous impartiality of the scientist with his criminal indifference to the destiny of his discoveries) is nothing more than a necessary myth of the ruling classes. That is why he must not confuse a concern with truth—which characterizes all serious scientific effort—with the myth of this neutrality.

On the other hand, in trying to understand reality, the critical and careful student cannot attempt to domesticate it to suit his own ends. What he wants is the truth of reality and not the submission of reality to his own truth. We cannot respond to the myth of the neutrality of science and the impartiality of the scientist with the mystification of truth, but rather with a respect for that truth. In effect, at the moment when one is seduced by this falsification of reality, one ceases to be critical. And the action resulting from such an uncritical or false knowledge cannot bear good fruit. So the student must be critical and involved, rigorous toward truth. This does not mean that his analysis must attain a definite or definitive profile of the social reality—because among other reasons, for reality to exist, it must be becoming.

This vigilant attitude characterizes the critical student, the student who is not satisfied with misleading appearances. He knows well that knowledge is not something given or finished, but a social process that demands the transforming action of human beings on the world. For this reason he cannot accept that the act of knowing would grow out of a simple narration of reality, even less—and this is worse—that it grows out of a proclamation that what exists is what must exist. Quite to the contrary, he wants to transform reality so that what is happening in a given manner begins to happen in another manner.

IDAC: If we consider the masses only on the level of their concrete context without permitting their movement toward a critical examination of that context, will they necessarily be condemned to a reformist option?

Freire: Insofar as they don't account for the subjectivity-objectivity dialectical unity, we cannot understand this very evident fact: the dominated classes' state of being cannot be understood as an isolated thing; it must be seen in its dialectical relationship to the ruling class. The dominated classes' tendency to reformist solutions is sometimes attributed to a sort of natural incapacity. Actually, however, the dominated classes become reformist in their dealings with the ruling classes. This happens in the concrete situation where they find themselves. Immersed in the alienation that constitutes their daily life, they do not spontaneously arrive at a self-consciousness in the sense of "class for itself."

IDAC: Isn't it fair to say that this is precisely the role of the revolutionary party?

Freire: In the last analysis, this is one of the fundamental jobs of any revolutionary party that is involved in attempts at a conscious organization of the oppressed classes, so that going beyond the stage of "class in itself" they can arrive at "class for itself." One of the basic aspects of this task rests on the fact that the relationships between revolutionary party and the oppressed classes are not relationships between one side that brings historical consciousness and another side, void of consciousness, arriving on the scene with an empty consciousness. If it were so, the role of the revolutionary party would be the transmission of consciousness to the dominated classes and this transmission would signify filling up their consciousness with the consciousness of their class. Actually, however, the dominated social classes are not void of consciousness, nor is their consciousness an empty depository. Manipulated by the ruling classes' myths, the dominated classes reflect a consciousness that is not properly their own. Hence, their reformist tendency. Permeated by the ruling class ideology, their aspirations, to a large degree, do not correspond to their authentic being. These aspirations are superimposed by the most diversified means of social manipulation. All this throws out a challenge to the revolutionary party. It unquestionably calls them to play a pedagogical role.

IDAC: One has to be aware, however, that attributing a pedagogical role to a revolutionary party carries with it the danger of a manipulation of the masses.

Freire: This danger exists; that's true. But we have to remember that the pedagogy of a revolutionary party can never be the same as that of a reactionary party. In the same way, the methods of the revolutionary party must necessarily be different. The reactionary party must, of necessity, avoid by all means the creation of class consciousness among the oppressed. The revolutionary party, on the contrary, finds this to be one of their most important tasks.

Finally, while it seems necessary to me to affirm that while analyzing the role the theoretical context can play in the critical radicalization of the process of awareness—which is verified in the concrete context—I don't want to say that the revolutionary party has to create in every historical situation theoretical contexts, as if these were revolutionary schools to prepare people to make the revolution. I've never claimed this. What I did say, and I repeat it here now, is that the revolutionary party that refuses to learn with the masses of people (and by so refusing breaks the dialectical unity between "teach" and "learn") is not revolutionary. It has become elitist; it forgets a fundamental point of Marx in his third thesis on Feuerbach: "The educator himself needs education."

IDAC: Let's talk for a moment, if you will, about this word that is constantly associated with you, *conscientization*. It has become the object of all sorts of ambiguous interpretations and distortions. Some wonder if the ruling classes cannot themselves "conscientize the people." Others, working at so-called revolutionary actions with the masses, also claim this word for themselves. Finally, many see conscientization as a sort of magic wand capable of "healing" social injustice by simply changing the conscience of men and women. Could you, one more time, clear up these mystifications and reconstitute for us the real content of conscientization?

Freire: To begin with I must say that it's impossible to correctly envisage conscientization as if it were an intellectual hobby or the constitution of a rationality separated from the concrete. Conscientization, which is identified with cultural action for freedom, is the process by which in the subject-object relationship (already so often mentioned in this conversation) the subject finds the ability to grasp, in critical terms, the dialectical unity between self and object. That is why we reaffirm that there is no conscientization outside of praxis, outside of the theory-practice, reflection-action unity.

As a demythologizing engagement, however, conscientization cannot be utilized by the ruling social classes. That is the case simply because they are the ruling classes. Cultural action, which such classes can develop, is necessarily that which, in mystifying the reality of consciousness, mystifies the consciousness of reality. It would be naive to expect the ruling classes to put into practice or even stimulate a form of action that would help the dominated classes see themselves as such. It must be said again that this is something that the revolutionary avant-garde must do, presupposing, of course, that they will not fall into the petite-bourgeois temptation of mechanical objectivism. Really, for these mechanical objectivists, the dominated classes *are just there*, as objects, to be freed by them in their role as subjects in revolutionary action. The process of liberation is, for them, something mechanical. Thus their willfulness. Thus their magical confidence in military action dichotomized from political action. That is why it is easier for them to accomplish a hundred dangerous activities, even though these may be void of political significance, than to engage in a dialogue with a group of peasants for ten minutes.

But we must also point out that conscientization cannot escape, by chance, from the limits historical reality imposes on it. That is, the effort of conscientization is not possible with a mistrust of historical viability. Sometimes it happens that the people's action, moving toward the demasking of oppressive structures of a given society, though partial, is not the political expression of historical viability. In other words, it can happen that the masses of the people comprehend the immediate reasons that explain a particular event, but that they do not grasp, at the same time, the relationship between this event and the total picture in which they participate—where the historical viability is found. In such a case, against event B, action A may not be the adequate action from the point of view of the totality. This would be the case, for example, of an action that though valid politically for a certain local area, would be inadequate in regard to the demand of the total national situation.

IDAC: This observation on the difficulty of grasping the total picture contained in the historical viability and organizing the diverse elements that constitute the totality seems fundamental and basic to us. Actually, to ensure their domination, the ruling classes need to divide the oppressed, pitting one against the other. Thus, in the United States, in the beginning of the liberation movement among the blacks, the principal enemy was simply the white, while at the same time the white workers made up one of the most racist groups in American society. The same phenomenon is seen, with a few different elements present, in the clash one observes in Latin America between the immediate interests of the urban-industrial proletariat and the demands of the peasantry. This is the case, while quite evidently the deepest interest of the two would be served in the identification of the principal common enemy. We see the escape from this fragmentary and partial vision as lying in the direction of the oppressed masses taking to themselves a class consciousness. How do you see this process?

Freire: I'll begin responding to that by reiterating that since it cannot be an atomized, spontaneous, or paternalistic "something to do," the work of conscientization demands from those who consecrate themselves to it a clear perception of the totality-partiality relationship, tactic and strategy, practice and theory. This work demands a no less clear vision than the revolutionary avant-garde must have of its own role, of its relationships with the masses of people. In these relationships, the avant-garde must be careful not to fall either into liberalism and lack of organization or into bureaucratic authoritarianism. In the first instance, they wouldn't be able to conduct a revolutionary process. They would dissolve into dispersed actions. In the second situation, in smothering the people's capacity for conscious action, they would transform those people into simple objects to be manipulated. In both cases, nothing present resembles conscientization.

Let's analyze now how the masses of people could go beyond this stage of "consciousness of the necessities of class" where they naturally find themselves, to attain the stage of class consciousness. The dialectical gap between these two stages is an unquestionable challenge to the revolutionary avant-garde. This dialectical gap is the ideological space where the dominated classes are found in their historical experience between the moment in which as a "class in itself" they act in a fashion that is out of accord with both their being and the moment when as a "class for itself" they become aware of their own historical mission. It is only at that latter moment that their needs are defined as class interests.

And there we are confronted with a difficult problem. On the one hand, class consciousness doesn't spontaneously engender itself separated from revolutionary praxis. On the other hand, this praxis implies a clear consciousness of the historical role played by the dominated classes. Marx underlined, in *The Holy Family*, the conscious action of the proletariat in the abolition of themselves as class by the abolition of the objective conditions that constitute that class.

Actually, class consciousness demands a class practice, which in turn gives birth to a knowledge at the service of class interests.

While the ruling class, as such, constitutes and reinforces self-consciousness in the exercise of economic, political, and sociocultural power which they impose on the dominant class, aligning it to their positions, this dominated class cannot attain its self-consciousness except by revolutionary praxis. In this process the dominated class becomes "class for itself," and in moving then in accord with their being, not only do they begin to know in a different way what they knew before, but they also begin to know what before they did not know. That is why class consciousness, not being a pure psychological state or a simple sensitivity on the part of the classes to detect what opposes their needs and interests, always implies a class knowledge. This knowledge is nontransferable. It is born in and through action on reality.

Going beyond this dialectical gap and demanding a revolutionary pedagogy, requires that the relationship between revolutionary party and dominated classes be verified in such a way that the party (as the critical consciousness of the masses of the people) does not block the process of class criticism.

IDAC: We can perhaps end this conversation by coming back to the problem of the organization of the revolutionary party. Can you systematize for us your criticism of forms of political action that are based on a mistrust of the creative and conscious participation of the masses of people and that grow out of—as you have already said—a petite-bourgeois concept of the relationship between the avant-garde and the masses?

Freire: I believe that one of the most difficult problems confronting a revolutionary party in the preparation of its militant cadres consists in rising above the canyon between the revolutionary option formulated verbally by the militants and the practice that is not always really revolutionary. The petite-bourgeois ideology that has permeated them in their class conditions interferes with what should be their revolutionary practice. This then becomes contradictory in relationship to their verbal expression. It's in this sense that methodological errors are always an expression of an ideological vision. For example, insofar as they keep within themselves the myth of the natural incapacity of the masses, their tendency is one of mistrust, of refusing dialogue with those masses, and of holding the idea that they are the only educators of the masses.

In so behaving, all they do is reproduce the dichotomy—typical of a class society—between teaching and learning in which the ruling class "teaches," and the dominated class "learns." They refuse, therefore, to learn with the people. They start giving prescriptions, "depositing" revolutionary knowledge. Because of all this, I'm convinced that the effort to clarify the process of ideologizing must make up one of the necessary introductory points in every seminar for preparing militants, simultaneously with the exercise of dialectical analysis of reality. In thus proceeding, the seminar becomes an occasion by which the participants— having been invited to overcome their naive and partial vision of reality, replacing it by a vision of the totality—engage also in a process of ideological clarification. They realize that dialogue with the people, in cultural action for freedom, is not a formality but an indispensable condition in the act of knowing—if our action is authentically revolutionary. They become aware that it is impossible, this dichotomy between the militant intent, which is political, and their methods, techniques, and processes through which the intent is translated into practice.

The political option of the militant determines the route that leads to its expression. There will always be radical differences between the leftist and the rightist militants in the use to which they can put even a slide projector. Many of the obstacles on the road of correct political-revolutionary action are rooted in the contradictions between revolutionary option and the use of methods that correspond to a practice of domination.

If my option is revolutionary, it is not possible for me to consider people as the object of my liberating act. If, however, my option is reactionary, the people will only be, as far as I'm concerned, a simple tool for my active preservation of the status quo, within which I am only interested in bringing about a few reforms. Political-revolutionary action cannot imitate political-dominative action. Enemies because of their goals, these two forms of action are set against each other not only by the practical consequences of chosen methods but also by the use they make of the aids and alliances serving them.

NOTES

1. This interview was carried out by the Institute of Cultural Action (IDAC) in Geneva, 1973.
2. Karl Marx, *The Holy Family*.
3. *Pedagogy of the Oppressed* (New York: Seabury Press, 1970).

CHAPTER THIRTEEN

An Invitation to Conscientization and Deschooling

A dialogical relationship is a sign of the cognitive act, in which the knowing object, mediating the knowable subjects, gives itself over to a critical revelation.[1]

The significance of seeing this dialogical relationship becomes clear whenever we take an epistemological cycle as a totality, rather than splitting it into one stage for acquiring existing knowledge and another stage for discovery or the creation of new knowledge. This dialogical relationship is similar "to the highest function of thinking—a heuristic activity of consciousness."[2]

In both stages of this epistemological cycle, a critical and curious posture is required of the knowable subjects, in light of the object of their knowledge, a critical posture that will always be negated when (in breaking the dialogical relationship) that dilemma of pure transference of knowledge is established, the dilemma by which knowing is no longer an act of creating and re-creating, but an act of "consuming."

"An invitation to conscientization and deschooling," once changed into magical or quasi-magical words, independent of Ivan Illich's or my wishes, are the precise words that bring us together. As a result of seeing them as objects of our critical curiosity, we can analyze their real meaning.

Nevertheless, there are specific goals for our analytical efforts and these serve as a point of departure for our common reflections and should be addressed by us.

Since the available space in an essay does not match the breadth of the task now facing us, I should begin at once. And to do this I should distance myself from the object of my reflection—the process of conscientization. I'll begin by asking myself a few questions. It seems to me that the first question in this self-inquiry is partly one of self-reintegration, centered on the very word *conscientization*, originating in the word *consciousness*. Comprehension of the process of conscientization and its practice is directly linked, then, to one's understanding of consciousness in its relations with the world.[3]

Were I to put myself in an idealist's frame of mind, splitting consciousness and reality, I would be submitting the latter to the former, as though reality were constituted by consciousness. Then, the transformation of reality would take place by a transformation of consciousness. Were I to put myself in a mechanistic frame of mind, setting up a similar dichotomy between consciousness and reality, I would be looking upon consciousness as a mirror that only reflects reality. In either case, I would be denying the conscientization that exists only when I not only recognize but also experiment with the dialectic between objectivity and subjectivity, reality and consciousness, practice and theory.

One's entire consciousness is always an awareness of something toward which one has some intention.

Human self-consciousness implies a consciousness of things, a concrete real world where people see themselves as historical beings in a reality they learn through their capacity for thought.

Knowledge of reality is essential for developing self-consciousness and a subsequent increase of knowledge. But if it's to be authentic, this act of knowing always requires the unveiling of its object. This does not take place in that dichotomy between objectivity and subjectivity, action and reflection, practice and theory.

While one is in the act of revealing the social reality in the process of conscientization, one must apprehend the real world, not as something that only exists, but as something that is to be, something that is being. But if one's reality is merely existence, and if reality is not within one's control, the interplay between permanence and change will only be the result of human experience on reality.

Reality thus requires one to discern the *raison d'être* of this experience—the goals, objectives, methods, and interests of those who command it. Whom does reality serve? Whom does it hurt? One needs to see, finally, that this is only a version of experience, not the only experience or an absolute destiny. In theoretical practice, the unveiling of social reality does not necessarily imply seeing it as a suffering reality that always emanates from a certain human experience. But its transformation, whatever it may be, cannot be verified outside experience.

If there is no conscientization without a revelation of objective reality, such a revelation is not enough in itself to assure a true conscientization, even though it may be a knowable object for the subjects involved in its process, and even though they may have a new perception of reality. Just as the epistemological cycle does not end at the stage of existing knowledge because it extends to the stage of creating new knowledge, conscientization cannot stop at the stage of revealing reality. It becomes authentic when we experience the revelation of the real world as a dynamic and dialectical unity with the actual transformation of reality.

I feel I should make a few more points. One would be a self-criticism, based on my *Education as Practice of Liberation*, for thinking that in the process of conscientization the moment of revealing a social reality is a kind of psychological motivation for its transformation. Obviously my mistake was not in recognizing the fundamental importance of knowing the real world in the process of its transformation. My mistake was that I did not consider the polarities—knowledge of reality and transformation of reality—in their dialectic. It was as though to unveil reality guaranteed that it was already being transformed. I said, in passing, in *Pedagogy of the Oppressed* and *Cultural Action for Freedom* that this is no longer my position regarding the problem of conscientization. The praxis that mediates these two books has taught me to see what I hadn't seen before. But, above all, it's my more incidental texts—interviews and small essays, such as "Education, Liberation, and the Church"—that inform my recent experience.[4] When I reconsider this problem, what I now know indicates a different approach from that espoused in *Education as Practice of Liberation*.

Considering my present and often more pronounced experience, I am becoming aware of this kind of mistake in some of my earlier activities and also from pedagogues who don't see the political dimensions and implications of their pedagogical practice. They speak of a conscientization that's strictly pedagogic, distinct from that of the politicians. This would be a conscientization generated in the intimacy of their rather aseptic seminars, having nothing to do with any commitment to political order.

Whether this is done ingenuously or astutely, separating education from politics is not only artificial but dangerous. To think of education independent from the power that constitutes it, divorced from the concrete world where it is forged, leads us either to reducing it to a world of abstract values and ideals (which the pedagogue constructs inside his consciousness without even understanding the conditioning that makes him think this way), or to converting it to a repertoire of behavioral techniques, or to perceiving it as a springboard for changing reality.

In fact, it is not education that molds society to certain standards, but society that forms itself by its own standards and molds education to conform with those values that sustain it. Since this is not a mechanical process, a society that structures education to benefit those in power invariably has within it the fundamental elements for its self-preservation.

The idea of education as a springboard for changing reality arises, in part, from an incomplete understanding of the above mentioned epistemological cycle. The idea is rooted in the second stage, where education functions as an instrument for self-preservation. It is as though defenders of such an idea were saying, "If education preserves itself, this is because it can change what it preserves." They forget that the forces that mold education so that it is self-perpetuating would not allow education to work against them. This is the reason any radical and profound transformation of an educational system can only take place (and even then, not automatically or mechanically) when society is also radically transformed.

This does not mean, however, that those educators who want and, even more so, are committed to the radical or revolutionary transformation of their society can do nothing. They have a lot to do, and without resorting to prescriptive formulas, they should determine their goals and learn how to reach them according to the concrete historical conditions under which they live.

They should clearly recognize their limitations and accept them gracefully and thus avoid falling into either an annihilating pessimism or a shameless opportunism.

For example, under certain historical circumstances, educators may not be able to participate directly in one or another aspect of the revolutionary transformation of their society, but this does not invalidate their less active role so long as their role is historically viable for them.

Throughout history one does what is historically possible and not what one would want to do.

Thus we recognize the necessity for an increasingly lucid understanding of their goals (which are political) and an understanding of their limitations so that, when possible, they can successfully confront this temptation of oscillating pessimism or opportunism.

This is always a difficult existential moment. Often, it is just when educators reach this point that they hear about conscientization. For various reasons (not understanding their goals, for instance) they approach conscientization as people who continue to listen passively, not as people who appropriate its real meaning. So they mystify the process of conscientization, giving it powers that it does not really have.

Sooner or later, though, the magic vanishes, taking away any naive hope that fed it, as well. When frustrated, rather than rejecting this mystification, these educators reject their role as subjects in the transformation of reality and join the ranks of mechanists.

My own experience has been teaching me how difficult it is, in essence, to bridge the gap between subjectivity and objectivity, to be *in* the world *with* the world without falling into the temptation of making one or the other an absolute. How difficult it is, really, to apprehend subjectivity and objectivity in their dialectical relationships.

Hence one focus of my efforts (perhaps the preponderant one) is turning myself into a tramp of the obvious, becoming the tramp of demystifying conscientization.

In playing the part of this vagrant, I have also been learning how important the obvious becomes as the object of our critical reflection, and by looking deeply into it, I have discovered that the obvious is not always as obvious as it appears.

Hence, my emphasis (often frustrating for my audiences), is not so much on the analysis of methods and techniques in themselves but on the political character of education, which can never be neutral.

If I can convince myself of the impossibility of this neutrality, not only through hearsay but by proving it through my experience, I can then perceive the relation between methods and their ends, in fact, the same relation that exists between tactics and strategy. Accordingly, I consider my methods, not as absolutes, but rather as the means to an end in whose pursuit they make and remake themselves.

Perhaps this is a mystification of methods and techniques and, indeed, a reduction of conscientization to certain methods and techniques used in Latin America for adult literacy. This would partly account for some of the statements I hear characterizing conscientization as a kind of tropical exoticism, a typically Third World entity. People speak of conscientization as an inviable goal for "complex societies," as though the Third World nations were not complex in their own way.

Without wishing to reanalyze the presence of the Third World in the body of the First and the presence of the First in the intimacy of the Third, I would simply like to emphasize that since it is a human phenomenon, conscientization is not merely a Third World privilege.

All of us are involved in a permanent process of conscientization, as thinking beings in a dialectical relation with an objective reality upon which we act. What varies in time and space are the contents, methods, and objectives of conscientization. Its original source is that point far off in time that Teilhard de Chardin calls "*Huminisation*," when human beings made themselves capable of revealing their active reality, knowing it and understanding what they know.

The problem, then, is not whether conscientization is viable for complex societies, but the distaste and disrespect of those societies for conscientization, their refusal to transplant its different forms of action from one part of the world to another historical space. It's not so important that this other historical space also belongs to the Third World. As a Third World man, I know very well the power of transplanting ideas, a practice that is ideologically alienating and benefits the dominating group. I have always been against this type of transplant and I would not defend it today.

Yet beyond a distaste for transplanting ideology there is another problem: the bureaucratization of conscientization, which in losing its dynamism and thus fossilizing, ends up transforming conscientization into a sort of rainbow of recipes—another mystification.

I shall conclude this admittedly incomplete review of our theme (one to which I have well, or otherwise, dedicated myself for a long time). Even though it's incomplete, I believe this review meets our main objective: to provoke commentary and questions that will expand these issues.

I will only add that what I have learned through my experience has in no way diminished those basic, youthful convictions derived from my first experiences in my country: a belief in a permanent search for knowledge. What I have learned has actually reinforced my convictions and helped me replace my naiveté with a more critical view of certain problems found in the challenge that new human realities have provoked in me.

NOTES

1. This text was previously published by ROSC (Geneva: World Council of Churches, 1975).

2. Álvaro Vieira Pinto, *Ciência e existência* (Rio de Janeiro: Paz e Terra, 1977), p. 363.

3. See chap. 12, "A Conversation with Paulo Freire."

4. See chap. 10, "Education, Liberation, and the Church."

Rethinking Critical Pedagogy:
A Dialogue with Paulo Freire

Macedo:* *What factors led you to your constant preoccupation with adult literacy, particularly the literacy of the oppressed?*

Freire: From a very young age I felt extremely attached to educational practice. When I was a young man, I accepted a position as a high school teacher of the Portuguese language. Teaching and studying Portuguese syntax fascinated me. Of course, at that time I taught youths whose families were very well-to-do.

My interests were studying the Portuguese language, and Portuguese syntax in particular, along with certain readings I did on my own in the areas of linguistics, philology, and the philosophy of language, which led me to general theories of communication. I was especially interested in the issues of meaning, linguistic signs, and the real need for intelligibility of linguistic signs between subjects conversing with one another for authentic communication to take place. These issues were my main intellectual preoccupations when I was nineteen to twenty-two years old. Another important influence was my wife, Elza. (We now have seven grandchildren.) Elza influenced me enormously.

Thus, my linguistics studies and meeting Elza led me to pedagogy. I began to develop certain pedagogical ideas along with historical, cultural, and philosophical reflections. As I was developing these ideas, however, I had to confront the very dramatic and challenging social realities of my childhood home, the Brazilian northeast. I had had an extremely difficult upbringing because of the economic situation of my family. Now as a young man, working with laborers, peasants, and fishermen, I once more became aware of differences among social classes.

*Translator of this book, Donaldo Macedo, is here the interviewer.

175

As a child I had associated with working-class children and peasants. As an adult I again associated with adult laborers, peasants, and fishermen. This new confrontation was much less naive, and more than any book, it led me to understanding my personal need to delve more deeply into pedagogical research. It also motivated me to learn from the adult educational practice in which I was involved.

I found literacy to be the most important issue, since the level of illiteracy in Brazil continued to be extremely high. Moreover, it seemed to me profoundly unjust that men and women were not able to read or write. The injustice that illiteracy in itself implies involves more serious implications, such as the castration of illiterates in their inability to make decisions for themselves, to vote, and to participate in the political process. This seemed absurd to me. Being illiterate does not preclude the common sense to choose what is best for oneself, and to choose the best (or the least evil) leaders.

I remember clearly that these injustices used to touch me, and they took up a lot of my time during my reflections and studies. One day, after considerable experience in the field of adult literacy, through debates and discussions geared toward people's views of their reality (and not my point of view), I began to develop a series of techniques that involved the meetings I used to conduct between parents and teachers in reference to the school and children. In Brazil this is called parent and teacher circles. For a long time I concentrated on advancing the techniques I developed in these encounters; I tried to see these meetings as forums for critical thinking about what is real and concrete. I continued this work for a long time without writing anything down (thus reflecting the oral quality of my culture). Then I began to question. Why not do something that would follow the same principles, the same critical vision, and the same pedagogy I had been using to debate issues like discipline? What is discipline? What is the relation between freedom and authority? What is the relation between the father's authority and the child's freedom? Why should children not begin to read by rote, sounding out the A B C's? In fact, using the sentence as a point of departure, they should begin with the totality of the word as a whole, and not the minimal part that is the grapheme. I asked, Why not write about the same themes I have been putting into practice when I talk with my adult students? What is underdevelopment? What is nationalism? What is democracy? Why not do the same thing when teaching people to read words?

After formulating these questions, I spent time investigating them until I found a way to teach. It is significant that you asked me this question because I don't think the North American reader has had any information concerning the development of my pedagogical thinking.

Macedo: *When you speak about your reencounter with the peasants, you highlight the notion that we have a lot to learn from peasants. Could you discuss this learning process in more detail?*

Freire: Of course we have a lot to learn from the peasants. When I refer to peasants, my emphasis is on our need to learn from others, the need we have to learn from learners in general. I have continually insisted that we must learn from peasants because I see them as learners at a particular moment in my educational practice. We can learn a great deal from the very students we teach. For this to happen it is necessary that we transcend the monotonous, arrogant, and elitist traditionalism where the teacher knows all and the student does not know anything. Obviously, we also have to underscore that while we recognize that we have to learn from our students (whether peasants, urban workers, or graduate students), this does not mean that teachers and students are the same. I don't think so. That is, there is a difference between the educator and the student. This is a general difference. This is usually also a difference of generations.

The issue is again political. For me it is also ideological. The difference between the educator and the student is a phenomenon involving a certain permanent tension, which is, after all, the same tension that exists between theory and practice, between authority and freedom, and perhaps between yesterday and today.

When educators are conscious of this tension and this difference, they must be constantly alert to not letting these differences become antagonistic. What we have to do is to live each day with the learners and cope with this tension between us—a tension that is reconcilable. Recognizing this situation as reconcilable, and not antagonistic, qualifies us as democratic educators, not elitists and authoritarians.

The more we live critically (this is what I would call a radical pedagogy in Giroux's sense[1]), the more we internalize a radical and critical practice of education and the more we discover the impossibility of separating teaching and learning. The very practice of teaching involves learning on the part of those we are teaching, as well as learning, or relearning, on the part of those who teach.

I can experience others in a real learning situation where the object of knowledge becomes a knowable subject, rather than a possession. This kind of situation mediates the knowable subjects, the educators and the learners. It is impossible to experience and appreciate someone in this concrete relationship if the educator and the learner do not know about one another, and if they do not teach one another.

It is along these lines of thought that I usually and categorically argue that we must learn from the peasants. If there are teachers who believe that they never need to learn from their university students, you can imagine what they say in reference to learning from a peasant. Their elitism distances them from peasants and laborers to such a degree that they often find my views on this issue to be rather demogogic or ignorant. But they aren't. In brief, I think that in a rigorous understanding of the process of knowing, seeing this as a social process (not merely an individual moment detached from the total process), it is impossible to separate teaching from learning.

Macedo: *You are often perceived as a thinker who operates outside the status quo. Do you think that departing from the system makes your thinking more creative and critical?*

Freire: I have been trying to think and teach by keeping one foot inside the system and the other foot outside. Of course, I cannot be totally outside the system if the system continues to exist. I would be totally outside only if the system itself were transformed. But it is not transformed because, in truth, it goes on transforming itself. Thus, to have an effect, I cannot live on the margins of the system. I have to be in it. Naturally, this generates a certain ambiguity, not just for me, but also for people like you, Giroux, Carnoy, and Berthoff[2]. This is an ambiguity from which no one can escape, an ambiguity that is part of our existence as political beings.

What is the nature of this ambiguity? In terms of tactics, we all have one foot inside the system, and strategically we have the other foot outside the system. That is, from the point of view of my dream and objective, I am strategically outside the system trying to pull my other foot outside! And with this other foot, of course, I am inside the system.

This ambiguity is often risky. That's why many people keep both their feet squarely inside the system. I know people who sometimes slowly try to place their right foot outside, but they are immediately overcome by fear. They see other people who have stepped outside and are punished. This is the case with Giroux, who was denied tenure because he had firmly stepped outside the system with his right foot. I don't doubt that many people, who were trying (and had even declared themselves) to be outside the system, ran back and plunked both feet inside after learning of Giroux's painful experience. These people have resolved their ambiguity. They have assumed a traditional posture. I love and admire Giroux because he continues to keep his right foot outside!

Macedo: *You have talked about the relationship of subjectivity and the politics of education. Can you elaborate this theme a little more?*

Freire: The issues concerning subjectivity are similar to those concerning theory and practice and existence in general. These are issues that touch upon philosophical reflection throughout time. In a certain way these issues function in terms of how you view consciousness acting upon subjectivity. You have the possibility of falling into an idealism that might be pre-Hegelian or Hegelian, in that you have the power to create objectivity. You can also fall into an antagonistic view in which subjectivity would be only a pure abstraction, a copy of objectivity. That is, Marx takes a big leap in these idealist preoccupations. But I believe that many people under the Marxist banner subscribe to purely mechanistic explanations by depending on a fatalism that I sometimes, humorously, call liberating fatalism. This is a liberation given over to history. Hence, it is not necessary to make any effort to bring about liberation. It will come, no matter what. I don't believe in this fatalism, of course. I don't let myself fall into either type of subjectivism: neither the one that determines history nor the other that I call liberating fatalism.

I could be completely wrong, but even within a Marxist critical viewpoint, the problem of comprehending the role of subjectivity in history is a factor, a real problem that we must confront head-on by the end of the century. Subjectivity relates to the problems of freedom, the world's reconstruction, and revolution, a revolution that has to eliminate or, at least, legislate subjectivity so that it follows the designs of objective thinking. Right now it seems to me to be epistemologically incomprehensible. Therefore, for me, all of these issues now must be properly addressed by the end of this century—problems like the role of social movements and the issues of power. Because I am extremely concerned with and see a vital role for subjectivity and consciousness in the making of history, I now feel that in transforming society, the important task is not to take power but to reinvent power. Without falling into an idealistic view or a mechanical explanation of history, I think that education (which is not a tool for transformation) has a lot to do with the reinvention of power. Thinkers, educators, and scholars like Giroux in this country have a major function to perform. When I refer to Giroux, I also symbolically include a great number of other educators of his generation, as well as economists like Carnoy, who has attempted to surmount his earlier, less dialectical thought. Today, Carnoy is moving more and more toward views that I talked about in answering your question. You will also find the same issues in the books of Agnes Heller, an ex-student of Lukács[3]. In respect to these issues, I don't think I have much of a contribution to make, and I say this, not with false modesty, but with sadness. Nonetheless, I will continue trying to contribute to a greater understanding of these issues.

Macedo: *What are some of the political consequences of your thinking and educational practice?*

Freire: When I began my educational practice as a young man I was not clear about the potential political consequences. I thought very little about the political implications and even less about the political nature of my thinking and practice. Yet, the political nature of these reflections was and is a reality. The political makeup of education is independent of the educator's subjectivity; that is, it is independent if the educator is conscious of this political makeup, which is never neutral. When an educator finally understands this, she or he can never again escape the political ramifications. An educator has to question himself or herself about options that are inherently political, though often disguised as pedagogical to make them acceptable within the existing structure. Thus, making choices is most important. Educators must ask themselves for whom and on whose behalf they are working. The more conscious and committed they are, the more they understand that their role as educators requires them to take risks, including a willingness to risk their own jobs. Educators who do their work uncritically, just to preserve their jobs, have not yet grasped the political nature of education.

I remember well my first night after working in adult literacy in Racife. When I got home Elza asked me, "How was it?" And I told her, "Elza, I think that what I saw today, what I experienced today, in two or three years many people will be asking me, 'What is this, Paulo?' But possibly I will be jailed. And I think the possibility of jail is more likely." In fact, not three, but four years later I was jailed.

During that period I was still not totally clear about the political nature of education, and I think my first book, *Critical Consciousness for Education*, reveals this lack of political clarity. For instance, I was not even able to touch upon politics in this first book. I continue to study this book, though, since it represents a particular moment in my work. (I am, of course, not simply the last book I wrote. All my books reveal points of development in my thinking.) But this book contains naive assumptions that I feel I have transcended in my second and third books. All of my thinking and searching were and are really part of a political framework, without which my efforts would be senseless.

Macedo: *You mentioned that you were jailed. What were your experiences in jail?*

Freire: I was jailed for a short time after the coup in Brazil in 1964. Actually, there were other people who were jailed for a much longer time. I was jailed twice before I was exiled, for a total of seventy-five days.

This was an interesting experience for me, even though I am not a masochist. I don't like to suffer and I certainly would not enjoy experiencing this again. But I took advantage of the time in jail by thinking things over. Those days were a learning experience. Of course, I was jailed precisely because of the political nature of education. Now you might say, "Paulo, there were other people involved in adult literacy and they were not jailed." My response could be that they were not political. I could also say that they were political. The only difference is that their politics furthered the interest of the dominant class. This is the real difference. There are no neutral educators. What we educators need to know is the type of political philosophy we subscribe to and for whose interests we work. My political ideas, fortunately, did not benefit and continue not to benefit the interests of the dominant class.

Macedo: *After seventy-five days you were exiled?*

Freire: After those seventy-five days in jail I was taken to Rio de Janeiro for further questioning. And there I was told via the newspapers that I ought to be jailed again. My friends and family convinced me that it would be senseless for me to stay in Brazil. So I went into exile in Chile, and afterward I came to the United States. From here I went to Europe. In total, I spent about sixteen years in exile.

Macedo: *Did your experiences in exile have any influence on further development of your critical and pedagogical thinking?*

Freire: No one goes through exile peacefully. In the first place, nobody goes into exile by choice. Second, no one goes through a period of exile without being strongly marked by it. Exile touches you existentially. It envelops you as a being. It shakes you up physically and mentally. Exile magnifies your virtues and faults. And this is what exile did to me.

It was while in exile that I realized I was truly interested in learning. What I learned in exile is what I would recommend to all readers of this book: each day be open to the world, be ready to think; each day be ready not to accept what is said just because it is said, be predisposed to reread what is read; each day investigate, question, and doubt. I think it is most necessary to doubt. I feel it is always necessary not to be sure, that is, to be overly sure of "certainties." My exile was a long time of continuous learning.

Since I have been interested in learning since youth, once I found myself in a time of exile in particular spaces (Chile, Cambridge, Geneva, and La Paz), I began to think and question myself, thus treating these spaces and the time of exile as a great teacher.

One of the first lessons exile taught me was that I could not and should not make value judgments about other cultures. We Brazilians have a particular style: the way we walk down the street, the way we turn a corner, typical expressions, facial gestures, and so forth. Of course, our style is no better or worse than any other.

I learned in Chile that as a Brazilian I reacted differently to certain situations.

From youth I have been open to different cultures and this sense of openness has helped me learn a great deal as a teacher and educator, and it has helped me think and rethink my opinions, which are not necessarily transferable to other cultures. For instance, after my first month of work in Chile, a few things became rather obvious. Chileans, not I, had to design and implement their own forms of education. Second, I had to help them to the extent that I could. Third, I learned that I could only help them if I began to understand them better. And I could not understand them better without understanding their culture and history.

This was a great learning experience for me, repeated with more peace of mind and a more critical view in Africa, when I was invited to Guinea-Bissau, Cape Verde, Angola, and São Tomé and Príncipe. I did not visit these places with a prefabricated modesty, but a modesty deeply rooted in strong convictions. I had learned that the very nature of my task called for learning about others' cultures so that I could teach them a little of what I think is valid.

When you ask me if exile helped me to reexamine my reflections, I would cite some common examples, certainly not as a sign of erudition, but as an indication of the extent to which these cultural differences have had a direct influence on deepening my intellectual development.

After three weeks or so in Chile, I went for a walk down a street in Santiago with a Chilean friend, and with a typical Brazilian gesture I put my hand on his shoulder as we walked. Suddenly he began to feel uncomfortable. I sensed his uneasiness and he finally told me, "Paulo, just between us, I don't feel comfortable having a man's hand on my shoulder." I moved my hand, of course, and thanked him for letting me know how he felt. When I went home I wondered, "Is there something wrong with a culture that rejects an affectionate gesture?"

Then, years later, I visited Tanzania in Africa. During a class break, an African professor and friend of mine invited me for a walk through the campus. While we walked he suddenly grabbed my hand and put his fingers between mine as if we were lovers strolling through the gardens of the university. I felt terribly uncomfortable. As a Brazilian from the northeast, a culture profoundly *machista*, I could not have reacted in any other way. I could not accept that I was holding hands with another man. I had only experienced this with women.

When he let go of my hand for a moment, I quickly put both hands in my pockets in fear that he would grab my hand again. Later I wondered, "Paulo, is there something wrong with your own culture that rejects an affectionate gesture?"

This sort of thing seems not to be that significant, but I would like to point out to the readers of this book that seemingly trivial incidents are, in fact, very important because they involve our whole lives, our cultures, the distinctive features that distinguish man from the other animals. Culture extends history to the praxis of people. These trivial incidents, then, have proven to be fundamental to me, and the more I experience them, the more they help me to keep in touch with myself, while learning and reflecting.

One final point: You cannot imagine how much Amilcar Cabral's extraordinary perceptions into various cultures have touched me. Also, Gramsci has profoundly influenced me with his keen insights into other cultures.

Macedo: *Speaking of Cape Verde, in your book* Pedagogy in Process: Letters to Guinea-Bissau, *you touched upon the notion of reappropriation of one's culture. Do you think it is possible, as Amilcar Cabral has stressed, to re-Africanize the people of Cape Verde and Guinea-Bissau by using Portuguese, the language of the colonizer?*

Freire: When he talked about the re-Africanization of Cape Verdeans, Amilcar Cabral stressed what he also calls cultural identity. You cannot Africanize the people within their own culture, which is their identity, if their culture is fractured. Language is one of culture's most immediate, authentic, and concrete expressions. Thus, for me the re-Africanization of Guinea-Bissau and Cape Verde involves the total reappropriation of culture, which also includes their language. I say "reappropriation" because a certain appropriation by the people never ceased to exist. No colonizer can really castrate a people culturally, except through genocide. The colonial process brings with it an incredible and dialectical counteraction. That is, there is no colonial intervention that does not provoke a reaction from the people about to be colonized. I see this problem as political, ideological, and not merely linguistic. It implies political decisions on the part of the government and the party. But these political decisions also imply a series of administrative and economic consequences.

First, I think you will agree that it would be very foolish for the people of Cape Verde, Guinea-Bissau, São Tomé and Príncipe, and other countries to cut themselves off completely from the Portuguese language, just because it is the language of the colonizer. To renounce totally the positive aspects of Portuguese culture (refusing to read Portuguese authors, for instance) makes no sense. In their process to reestablish a relationship with these countries, the ex-colonizers should help point out the advantages Portuguese may offer. The question that needs to be posed is how to activate and formalize the use of the African native languages so they can gradually replace the colonizer's language in such fields as economics, politics, and finance.

I don't think you can translate overnight all of the necessary work (books, texts, documents) into Creole. These countries do not have the economic base to do this, without stopping the basic flow of goods. So these countries must confront this ambiguity. This is one of the most important problems regarding culture, but it cannot be met head-on at the sacrifice of other basic issues vital to the infrastructure.

These countries need to creolize in phases, starting with the first years of primary school through high school, so that people everywhere would feel free to express themselves in their native language without fear and without perceiving any elitist restriction. Indeed, they will come to terms with themselves to the degree that they speak their own language, not the colonizer's language. Moreover, I think there is a great risk when countries like Cape Verde and Guinea-Bissau choose a national language. I sympathize with all of the political difficulties that these new countries confront. These difficulties are much greater in Angola and Mozambique, however, where there is no Creole. How can the governments of Angola and Mozambique select one of the indigenous languages as the national language? To do this could possibly mean a rupture among various ethnic groups that might feel linguistically disenfranchised. This could even endanger the very process of revolution. Nonetheless, this is not the case with Guinea-Bissau and Cape Verde, where you have a Creole that cuts across ethnic differences.

The main problem is that these countries adopt Portuguese as the official language for technical, scientific, and political thinking. You have Cape Verdean children who have to learn geography, history, biology, math, and the social sciences in Portuguese. This should be a task for the national language, not the "official" language. This is like asking my children in Brazil to study the history of Brazil in English. You can see what a violation of the structure of thinking this would be: a foreign subject (such as English) imposed upon the learner for studying another subject. If a Cape Verdean child has difficulties learning the Portuguese language, you can imagine how difficult it would be to learn other subjects in Portuguese.

I think this kind of politics has to become more realistic within the next few years. Politicians have to be clear about language. They need to appreciate that language is not only an instrument of communication, but also a structure of thinking for the national being. It is a culture.

I think this is also your view, Donaldo, from what I have read in your writings. If these countries continue much longer to insist on using Portuguese as the official political and scientific language, this issue will once again become political because the Portuguese language will determine historical and scientific formation, penetrating with its ideology into the people's very being. Beyond this, in continuing to use Portuguese, there is yet another danger— elitism. Since they are educated by the colonizer and are thus very fluent in Portuguese, only the politicians and their children are bilingual. Only powerful families succeed in the educational system. Children of these families are the only ones who excel in exams and get good grades. They are the only ones who have access to science and technology. Thus, most children, the sons and daughters of peasants, will be excluded. And tomorrow the new generation of power will comprise only the children of the families in power today.

This will also establish a great social distance between most of the people and these children from families now in power, those who will be in the government tomorrow. In the final analysis, linguistic politics, a dimension of the politics of culture, will wind up deepening social class differences, creating an immense revolutionary contradiction.

Macedo: *What do you think of the idea that Creole is an antagonistic force? That is, Creole is a force that threatens the privileged and dominant position of the Portuguese language.*

Freire: I think you have touched upon a probable reason, perhaps at the subconscious level, why many good people in these countries continue to refuse to use Creole. This is just one reason. In truth, there is another, ideological justification for their refusal.

For many years, from childhood through adolescence, these very people who achieved liberation for their countrymen were marked by a socialization process in which the colonizers would not recognize Creole as an autonomous and beautiful language. On the contrary, the colonizers had to convince the people that the only valid language was Portuguese. They always emphasized that what the colonized spoke was an ugly and savage dialect. Obviously, the colonized people could not acculturate the colonizer, since in most cases they adapted to the colonizer's culture. Those in power are the ones who make other people fall in line. Those who do not have power must achieve it before they can begin to incorporate others within their cultural value system.

After centuries of hearing that Creole is ugly and not valid, people begin to believe this myth. I have heard many well-educated people in Africa tell me that Creole is not a language, that they have to maintain Portuguese because it is a superior langauge. I always used to point out to them that their assessment of Creole is a form of reproducing the dominant ideology, that of the colonizer, and that this is counter to the struggle for liberation.

These are the subconscious and ideological reasons for resisting Creole. But these reasons are often disguised. People stress that they need to advance technologically and scientifically because otherwise they jeopardize the struggle for liberation. It is as if the Creole language does not have all the preconditions to fulfill these tasks, particularly in the area of the modern sciences. None of this is true, Donaldo, you, yourself, know that this reasoning is false. First, there has never been a language that sprang up completely developed in all domains of communicative functions. A language can only develop when it is practiced in all domains and given opportunity to do so. When I was in Africa, I used to say that all of this involves the production force of the society. For example, today these so-called beautiful and advanced Europeans languages are seeking the means for dealing with the technological terminology developed by North Americans. When they cannot translate these terms, these European languages are forced to incorporate English terms like *stress* and *input*. In Brazil we say *esta estressado*. This does not mean that Brazilian Portuguese, French and other languages that have incorporated these English terms are inferior. These languages were forced to borrow these terms.

When my work was first issued in the United States, some people insisted that we put into an equivalent English phrase our concept of *conscientização* or "conscientization." I refused. Why not accept this term? I do not have to accept *stress*, but I have. Why do you not accept *conscientização?*

I think that a firm grasp of the nature of language would dispel these false notions about Creole. Creole has all the possibilities for developing and finding its own ways to express technological and scientific ideas. The main issue is to allow people to make and develop their own Creole. Creole cannot be systematized by anyone but the people who speak it.

Macedo: *There is a large body of literature in sociolinguistics on the interre-lationship of language and society, analyses of the role language plays in promoting and maintaining sex differentiation, analyses of language and ethnicity, and so on. How can these language variations be used as an antag-onistic force to challenge the privileged position of the so-called standard language?*

Freire: At a particular moment in the struggle for self-affirmation, when sub-ordinated to and exploited by the ruling class, no social group or class or even an entire nation or people can undertake the struggle for liberation without the use of a language.

At no time can there be a struggle for liberation and self-affirmation without the formation of an identity, and identity of the individual, the group, the social class, or whatever. And to the extent that conflicts increase, experience has taught us that individuals, groups, and social classes end up building walls behind which, in times of struggle or peace, they embrace their identity and protect it.

Without a sense of identity, there is no need for struggle. I will only fight you if I am very sure of myself. I am definitely not you. The reasoning process is similar for groups, even at a subconscious level. In this subconscious process, which the very nature of conflict involves, we do not even recognize the sig-nificance of our elaborating a particular language while we are consciously defending ourselves in the struggle for liberation. This is why colonized people need to preserve their native language. And the more sophisticated they make their language, the better it will be that the colonizer not understand it, and in this way they can use their language to defend themselves against the colonizer.

By way of example, I am in total sympathy with women's fantastic struggle, even though I cannot fight their battle. Although I am a man, I can feel like a woman, and I am not afraid to say this. But women's liberation is their struggle. They need to elaborate their own female language. They have to celebrate the feminine characteristics of their language, which they were so-cialized to despise and view as weak and indecisive. In the process of their struggle, they have to use their own language, not man's language. I believe these language variations (female language, ethnic language, dialects) are in-timately interconnected with, coincide with, and express identity. They help defend one's sense of identity and they are absolutely necessary in the process of struggling for liberation.

Macedo: *How would you characterize the interrelationships of language, culture, and thought?*

Freire: There may be times when these interrelationships do not exist. There is a certain relationship between thought and language as an expression of the actual process of thinking and the concreteness of the reality of the one who speaks, who thinks and speaks, and who speaks and thinks. We could even invent a new verb, "to speak-think" or "to think-speak."

In a certain context of temporal space this cultural being creates itself along with other beings, similar to the way I make myself relative to that which is not me, the very world that is not me. My language and thinking, I believe, are a dialectical unity. They are deeply rooted in a context. So if there is a change of context, it will not be enough to mechanically propagate a distinct form of thinking-speaking; it will have to come about by necessity. I think one of the tasks of critical education and radical pedagogy is to help the critical thinking-speaking process to re-create itself in the re-creation of its context. Instead of assuming that this re-creation takes place at only a mechanical level (this never happens), pedagogy should assume the role of helping to reformulate this thinking.

Take Cape Verde, for example. Cape Verde has been changing radically in the past six years or so because there is no context-object anymore, as there once most definitely was in relation to the context-subject, Portugal. Cape Verde has cut the false umbilical cord. Portugal used to think that there was an umbilical cord, but there never was. For there to be a real umbilical cord there had to be an existential-historical connection, and in the case of Cape Verde there was none. The connection was forced upon Cape Verdeans by the Portuguese. But, fortunately, the people have cut the cord.

What happens after the cut? Cape Verde begins to crawl in its infant experience of being itself. Cape Verde tries to find itself. What was thought-language before independence cannot stay the same: it would be too much out of sync. But you cannot artifically change the context to any great degree, either. That's why I admire Cape Verde's president, Artistides Pereira. He gave a speech in Praia in which he made an extraordinary statement that has a lot to do with our conversation now: "We made our liberation and we drove out the colonizers. Now we need to decolonize our minds." That's it exactly. We need to decolonize the mind because if we do not, our thinking will be in conflict with the new context evolving from the struggle for freedom.

This new historical context, which is intertwined with culture, can only be new to the degree that it no longer is colonized. Cape Verde has a different mentality and a different culture reemerging. The repressed native culture is beginning to reemerge. Certain cultural behavior patterns that were forbidden by the colonizers, including language, expressions of the world, poetry, and music, are reappearing. People walk without having to bow any longer. They now walk upright, looking up. There is a pedagogy of walking in this new behavior, walking freely. All of these issues constitute a new way of thinking and a new way of speaking. Now you can see the tremendous problem there would be if this new thinking were not to coincide with the existing language. A new thinking expressed in the colonizer's language goes nowhere.

Macedo: *With respect to your literacy work, a major concern in the so-called developed nations is that it seems not to be applicable to the non-Third World context. Could you address this issue, and possibly talk about the Third World context found within the First World, and how your educational proposals may be applied here?*

Freire: From my earliest travels throughout the world, including the First World, I have been asked these basic questions. I think, though, in the past few years this kind of questioning has diminished somewhat. First, let's talk about the issue of the Third World and the First World. From my experiences living in the United States (I was very happy in Cambridge, and I still remember Broadway, the street where I lived), I discovered the presence of the Third World in the First World, such as the ghettos in the United States. I also discovered vicious racial discrimination and linguistic chauvinism, which is a type of racism. I simultaneously found and lived this reality. I was also discriminated against (perhaps not as much as other foreigners, particularly immigrants, because many people knew me and my work). But sometimes I felt discriminated against. People thinking I was Spanish would be more courteous when I told them that I was Brazilian. I suppose that's because there were not many Brazilians in Cambridge!

Discovering the Third World in the First, I became aware of the obvious: the presence of the First World in the Third World, the ruling class. Here in the United States as elsewhere in the First World the situation is far more complex. Since the United States is not merely the First World, and since some educators, not I, say that my literacy approach is only applicable in the Third World context, they should at least apply my approach to their easily identifiable Third World.

The main problem is that these educators are dealing in the wrong issues when they say that Freire's proposals, even though they are interesting, have nothing to do with a complex society. The issues here should be defined differently. The educational proposals that I have been making for years basically derive from two rather obvious, nonsimplistic ideas.

First, education is a political act, whether at the university, high school, primary school, or adult literacy classroom. Why? Because the very nature of education has the inherent qualities to be political, as indeed politics has educational aspects. In other words, an educational act has a political nature and a political act has an educational nature. If this is generally so, it would be incorrect to say that Latin American education alone has a political nature. Education worldwide is political by nature. In metaphysical terms, politics is the soul of education, it's very being, whether in the First World or in the Third World. When a teacher studies a particular subject (when Giroux, for instance, analyzes the hidden curriculum), all instances of education become political acts. There is no way I or anyone else can contradict this. The political nature of education, then, is not Paulo Freire's exoticism from the Third World.

Second, in Brazil or wherever, whether working in literacy or postgraduate studies, education is a series of theories put into practice. We cannot escape this. Whether it be you here in Massachusetts or I in Brazil, no matter what we discuss (linguistics in your case, the relationship of educator and learner in my case), what seems to be most important is the object of knowledge posed for us as educators. Once we are involved in this educational practice, we are also engaged in a practice of knowing. We may be trying to learn a predetermined, existing knowledge, or we may be trying to create a knowledge that does not yet exist, like research. All these educational practices involve the act of knowing, throughout the world.

The issue to be defined now is what are our positions in these acts of knowing. What are our views in the theory of knowledge? How do we approach the object of knowledge? Do we own it? Do we carry it in our suitcases to distribute to our students? Do we use this object of knowledge to feed students or to inspire them to know? Do we stimulate students to assume the role of subjects, rather than the role of patients and recipients of our knowledge?

Well, these are not just Third World issues; they are universal issues. But I do not want to say that there are no limitations imposed by different cultures, politics, and ideologies. There are real limits on the democratic practice of knowing, in this country and elsewhere. Again, creative and critical educational experience is not an exoticism of the Third World.

In literacy, learners should assume the role of subjects in the very process of mastering their language. University students should assume the role of knowing subjects in the interchange between students who know and educators who also know. Obviously, teachers are not the only subjects who know.

The point of departure in this process of knowing educators and learners focuses on the expectations and stumbling blocks that learners confront in the learning process, not on the expectations and knowledge of the educator. Again, I would point out that this is not an exoticism from the Third World.

Beyond these arguments, I am thinking about the coherence of a political position within a pedagogical outlook, which is also political by nature, and therefore, a coherence of a theoretical posture within the practice of this theory.

Sometimes educators forget to recognize that no one gets from one side of the street to the other without crossing it! No one reaches the other side by starting from the same side. One can only reach the other side by starting from the opposite side. The level of my present knowledge is the other side to my students. I have to begin from the opposite side, that of the students. My knowledge is my reality, not theirs. So I have to begin from their reality to bring them into my reality. A teacher may say, "This is another romantic naivete of Paulo Freire." I insist, however, that there is no romanticism in these ideas. What we find here is an epistemological coherence with a political outlook.

There seem to be fewer questions about the validity of my educational theory and practice in the First World because intellectuals and committed educators in the United States, the U.K., and Europe are rigorously studying my work. Although they may not always agree with me, many see the viability of these ideas in the First World context. In the field of teaching English as a second language (ESL) here in the United States, there are a number of teachers and critical pedagogues who work along the general lines of my thinking. Also, Ann Berthoff and Aida Shaw incorporate my ideas in both their theories and practices. About five years ago, an interesting and voluminous book, *Learning with Freire*, was published in Germany, involving a longitudinal experiment on preschool education that incorporated my methods. In *Pedagogy of the Oppressed* and *Pedagogy in Process: Letters to Guinea-Bissau* I have stressed that my experiences should be re-created, not transplanted. In sum, my educational experiments in the Third World should not be transplanted to the First World; they should be created anew.

Macedo: *During an earlier discussion you mentioned that some of your educational theories are now being studied by physicists. Coincidentally, Richard Horsley, professor of theology at the University of Massachusetts, has said that he began to understand the New Testament better after reading* Pedagogy of the Oppressed. *Can you comment on the impact your educational theory is having in various fields of study?*

Freire: Throughout my life, especially after *Pedagogy of the Oppressed* was published in the United States, and after traveling all over the world, I have observed many educational practices that seem to be influenced somewhat by my thinking. I would say, then, there is a universal dimension to what I have been writing about education. I have the impression that *Pedagogy of the Oppressed* was born out of a long-lived experience. I insist on the affective domain of things, the humanistic and intuitive dimensions of the act of knowing. I never put feelings and emotions between parentheses. I only recognize them as I express them. This book was born through a marriage between me and the many parts of the world knowledge I had lived and experienced where I lived, and where I worked and taught with commitment, feelings, fear, trust, and courage. This book is radical, etymologically speaking. It came from the depths of fragments of Latin American history and culture, particularly those of Brazil. This book is saturated by time, history, and culture. And this, I believe, is how the book acquired its universality.

I do not think universality is possible without a vibrant community as a point of departure. We do not generalize without basing our generalizations on particulars. Before becoming universal, you are particular. You cannot leave the universal to reach the local. For me, whatever universality there is in *Pedagogy of the Oppressed* derives from the vigor and force of its locale. I had no pretentions or dreams of developing a universal theory with this book. The point is, though, the book contains certain issues that concern people universally. For example, I have received comments from many people in Asia and Africa, saying, "I read your book and now I better understand my own country." I will never forget a letter I received from a South Korean who told me he was reading my book secretly. (I do not even know how he was able to send me that letter.) He thanked me because my book was helping him understand his society better. I have received letters from other people in the Orient who spoke similarly. In one letter, a museum curator told me that he was really influenced by the third chapter of *Pedagogy of the Oppressed*.

I have also been told by mathematicians and physicists that they are highly influenced by my work. About a year and a half ago I was invited to be a reader in a doctoral dissertation committee for the Physics Department at the University of São Paulo. They told me they study my work quite carefully (not as a discipline, of course). And a student in that department presented a doctoral thesis titled, "How to Study Science in a Freirean Perspective."

In a general way, I have been studied by sociologists and theologians in the United States, Europe, and England.

There are issues in *Pedagogy of the Oppressed* that touch these various fields of knowledge. My discussions of these issues may not necessarily furnish answers, but they are challenging. They provoke a critical reflection on the part of physicists, mathematicians, anthropologists, artists, musicians, and others.

During a week-long seminar I was conducting at York University, England, a student came up to me and said, "Paulo, I am not enrolled in this seminar. I am an ex-student in the Music Department at this university. I'm a musician and a composer. I came here to tell you that I read *Pedagogy of the Oppressed* and that I was so moved by it that I wrote a musical version of *Pedagogy of the Oppressed*." I was so deeply touched by his remarks that I was struck silent from surprise. Then we shook hands. I gave him a hug and simply told him, "I am very happy." When I returned to Geneva and told my son, who is a very good classicial guitarist, he asked, "How come you didn't ask him to send me his piece so I could play it? I'd love to play *Pedagogy of the Oppressed!*" All I could tell him was how surprised and speechless I was.

Incidents like this keep on occurring. Like my other books, *Pedagogy of the Oppressed*, at a certain point in its trajectory, has left me. I find this very beautiful because books, like people, need to achieve their autonomy. Now, when I see *Pedagogy of the Oppressed* in bookstores, I almost say good morning to it!

Macedo: *In your theory, how can we talk about the critical appropriation of the dominant culture by the dominated people?*

Freire: This question is very critical. In the contradiction of the dominant and dominated, there is a cultural and class conflict. This conflict is such that the dominant will break the forces of the dominated and do all they can to anesthetize the self-consciousness of the dominated people, denying them the essence of their culture as something that exists in their experience and by which they also exist. Culture here is meant in the broadest sense, ranging from the way one walks to knowledge of the world, expressions of this knowledge, and expressions of this world through music, dance, and so on.

The dominant need to inculcate in the dominated a negative attitude toward their own culture. The former encourage the latter to reject their own culture by instilling a false comprehension of their culture as something ugly and inferior. Further, the dominant impose their way of being, talking, dancing, their tastes, even their way of eating. Speaking of eating, this is where the dominant impose less, precisely because they do not want to point out how much better they eat than those they dominate.

What happens when the dominated people finally realize their culture is not ugly as their dominators say? What happens when they see that their values are not so deplorable, that their presence in the world is not as despicable as the dominators say? In truth, the dominated are human beings who have been forbidden to be what they are. They have been exploited, violated, and violently denied the right to exist and the right to express themselves. This is true whether these dominated people represent a unique people, a social group (like homosexuals), a social class, or a particular gender (like women).

At a specific point in time, in this relationship of dominator and dominated, something snaps. And when more and more things snap, they bring about mobilization. Initially, this mobilization is minimal. But this mobilization keeps increasing as it takes on different issues in different contexts. Sometimes the dominators are more violent, intimidating the dominated people, making them suffer more. Yet, there comes a breaking point, and these breaking points add up, increasing in frequency, intensity, and quality. All of these breaking points are also moments of culture, by necessity. Dominated people could never learn how to fight if this were not a cultural experience. In the same sense, Amilcar Cabral clearly perceived that movements of liberation are, on the one hand, a cultural fact, and on the other hand, a factor of culture. The experiences of uniting, of sparking a different and forbidden speech, of discovering that this speech is valid (though forbidden), of seeing that this speech is beautiful (even though some say it is ugly): these experiences are cultural and belong to the culture of the dominated people. The more dominated people mobilize within their culture, the more they unite, grow, and dream (dreaming is also a part of culture), and the more they fantasize (fantasy is a part of culture involved with the act of knowing). Fantasy actually anticipates the knowledge of tomorrow. (I do not know why so many people belittle fantasy in the act of knowing.) In any case, all of these acts constitute the dominated culture that wants to liberate itself.

And what happens to the dominated culture when it strives for liberation? When it was merely the dominated culture, it was subject to indoctrination, and it was domesticated. But now, though still dominated, it wants to liberate itself. And in this process of wanting to liberate itself, it also discovers that the dominant culture, precisely because it is dominant, was forced to develop a series of analytical, and scientific strategies to achieve its own purposes. The dominant culture develops these strategies to analyze and explain the world in order to dominate. When the dominated culture perceives the need to liberate itself, it discovers that it has to take the initiative and develop its own strategies, as well as use those of the dominant culture. The dominated culture does this, not simply to suit itself, but to better fight against oppression. Then, one day, the elaborated culture at the service of the dominators ceases to be so, and a culture is re-created by the ex-dominated people for the benefit of a permanent liberation.

This seems to me to be a humanistic perspective, not idealistic, or cunning, or angelic. I refuse to reject this humanistic view.

You asked me this question, perhaps, because I said sometime in the past (I do not remember where) that in the process of liberation, the dominated can and must critically incorporate some of the dimensions of the dominant culture to serve as the very instruments of their own struggle.

Macedo: *In what ways have social movements (such as women's liberation, peace movements, the environmentalists), created a new mode of discourse for liberation?*

Freire: I think this question complements the one you asked earlier, dealing with subjectivity, a theme I consider politically relevant to the end of this century.

I remember, for instance, that during the beginning of the 1970s when I was in Europe, some people discussed social movements, like women's liberation and the ecology movement, just as they were beginning to take hold. And I recall that some people from the left showed very little respect for these movements. People said that movements would have no political significance because they did not identify social classes, only individuals within these classes. I thought that there was something ingenuous and dogmatic in criticizing these movements as inoperative, or mere distractions, or "escapisms."

I remember a couple, good friends of ours, who had recently returned to Brazil with whom I worked at the Institute for Cultural Action, which I established in Geneva. They were extremely critical of these movements. We discussed their criticisms, which seemed to me to be dogmatic and sectarian. And from that time onward, I felt that social movements constituted their own language as moments and movements of liberation.

For example, the ecologists emerged to defend the environment in a human and poetic language. By defending the environment, they are defending everyone. I used to say, "Sooner or later, they will overcome the dormant politics inherent in their movement." Social movements were born *already* political, even though their political nature was not always understood by the people involved. This political dimension (that goes well beyond the immediate scope of any movement) will amplify the objectives and language of liberation.

I see this as a worldwide phenomenon. But I also see something that is still not completely defined or delineated. These social movements began by judging the traditional behavior of the political parties to such an extent that political parties, in my opinion, revealed themselves as discredited entities to a large number of youths. While still in Europe, I was concerned about the political role played by social movements, and at the same time, I thought about their limitations at the political level. Social movements should not stop at personal and individual liberation. Yet, to put an act of liberation into practice takes an act of power. And an act of power, I repeat, should be reinvented, that is, re-created to function in the new spirit of these movements.

I thought that social movements would not have the means to reach formal power. If they were to become new political parties, for instance, they ran the risk of becoming traditional, as well. So the issue is, how can political parties approach social movements, and develop their own language? To what extent can these nonsectarian, nonauthoritarian political parties learn from these movements? I am speaking, not of the parties of the right (I am interested in studying the parties of the right, but I do not want to belong to them), but of the popular parties of the left. These parties need to approach social movements without attempting to overpower them. In approaching these movements, the leftist parties will, in a sense, enhance and complete themselves.

These were some ideas I had in Europe and that I intensely lived through when I returned to Brazil. There, I saw the force of family organizations and the grass-roots communities within the Catholic Church, which in the past fifteen years have had extraordinary repercussions and have sparked rereadings of the gospel.

Of course, there are those who do not like these rereadings, viewing them as communist and diabolic interventions. These rereadings are nothing like that. They involve a critical perspective where the gospel is reread from the point of view of those who suffer and those who make others suffer. Within this piece of political history in Brazil, I witnessed how a political party begins to emerge and constitute itself inside a social movement. The new political party of the Brazilian working class may disappear tomorrow, but for the moment it struggles to incarnate this reawakened spirit that's so important for dealing with the issues concerning the end of the century. This party has emerged from, and continues today to approach, social movements without trying to dominate them. In fact, this is why I have become a member of this party.

I am not sure whether social movements worldwide are creating their own discourse. (They should be, in my opinion, since one's own language plays an important role in the process of liberation.) What I do know is that these movements are a presence in the many attempts to re-create some societies.

For instance, the role of the ecologists in France is indisputable. They were enormously influential in the last elections leading to Mitterrand's victory. In Germany, they are also very important.

There are other examples as well that occasionally appear in complex societies like the United States, but they are marked by a kind of escapism. This escapism can be realistic, since the desire, need, and anguish to escape must be present for these movements to exist in the first place. If you have a movement involving five hundred thousand people, this proves there is some basic anxiety behind the escapism. But in Latin America escapist movements largely do not exist. In Latin America people need change, not escape. As I have said, I appreciate the need for escapist movements (some even create their own language, which is also escapist), but these movements have little influence.

No educator who dreams of a different society can dismiss social movements. One of our tasks is to try to understand social movements, and see how we can offer them concrete methods toward liberation.

Macedo: *In an earlier conversation with Judy Goleman and Neal Bruss [University of Massachusetts faculty members] you were asked to discuss what you like to do. Can you comment on this now?*

Freire: When Neal asked me this question, I felt excited, and I wanted very much to answer him but I did not have the time. Now, I will simply talk about what I like best, but let me add that what I am about to say should be understood in both intellectual and empathetic terms.

I really like to like and feel good about other people. I like to live, to live my life intensely. I am the type of person who loves his life passionately. Of course, someday I will die, but I have the impression that when I die, I will die intensely as well. I will die experimenting with myself intensely. For this reason I am going to die with an immense longing for life, since this is the way I have been living.

This is also the way I work in pedagogy. This is the way I make friendships, and the way I read a book. I cannot read a book disinterestedly. I cannot read a book that does not touch me or move me. So the first thing I must say about what I like to do is, I like to live!

For me, the fundamental thing in life is to work in life to create an existence overflowing from life, a life that is well thought-out, a created and re-created life, a life that is touched and made and remade in this existence. The more I do something, the more I exist. And I exist intensely.

Even though I like to love people and to live intensely, I may not treat all people well all the time. One might expect that in wanting to like people so much, I would always treat people well. It is possible sometimes that I treat others not so well. I have to accept this shortcoming as a fact of liking to live, of living passionately. Sometimes my passion to live, which is confused with the passion of knowing, leads me to do wrong to others. But these wrongs are involuntary.

Now, keeping in mind this notion of liking to live, I like a number of other things. I really love to chat. I put in "all-nighters" when conversing, remembering and reliving with friends past experiences that we lived through together. Two or three years ago, Elza and I entertained an old friend of ours at our house. This friend worked with me in Chile. She is an excellent sociologist, and I love her dearly. She is also a lover of life, like me. And like me, she loves *pisco*, a typical drink from her country. She brought me a bottle from Chile. I remember that we spent all night talking and drinking *pisco*. This was the kind of conversation where we talked about everything and anything, and everything was valid, our doubts, our laughter, our sadness, our memories, our happiness, our criticism toward what we did and did not do. We relived a portion of her life when she was very young in Chile, then a portion of my life when I worked in Chile and she was my assistant.

I love to do this type of thing, to chat with friends. My friends here in the United States do this whenever we can. I remember the many hours I spent two years ago in Boston, conversing with you and Henry Giroux. On my way to the United States I stop in Mexico, and spend time with friends there, talking and remembering. I do not feel that I waste time doing this. I learn a great deal from these chats. To me, these conversations are as rich as a planned seminar, and they can be as rigorous in their breadth. Back in Brazil, many times after a conversation with a friend on a tropical porch, I go home and write down some of the points made in our conversation, and I reflect upon them. For me, to converse with two, three, four, or more people is a way to read the world.

I love to eat. I do not know if you agree with me, but I think there is a certain connection with eating, liking to eat, sensuality, and creativity. I must confess that I am somewhat afraid of people who tell me that they do not like to eat. I become a little suspicious (except in cases of illness, of course). But I am suspicious of a person who simply prefers pills or plastic food to a good meal, like a Brazilian *feijoada,* or a Cape Verdean *catchupa* or a French dish. Now, it may be possible to exchange pills for food, and this would also be culture. Taste, after all, is cultural. But I live intensely and culturally to taste my food! I spent sixteen years in exile, with Elza helping me to survive by looking all over for things that tasted like home cooking.

For me, eating is a social act, like conversing. If I am by myself while eating, no matter how good the food, I will not enjoy it because I will feel somewhat limited. I need to eat with other people. Food mediates conversation.

I also like to drink a little. Not only fruit juices, which I adore, but I like to drink Brazilian *cachaça* or a good French, Chilean, or Californian wine. And I adore a good Portuguese wine.

I also love all kinds of music, not only the so-called classical music. At home when I am exhausted by my workload, a good piece reenergizes me. Vivaldi or the Brazilian, Villa-Lobos. Villa-Lobos takes me into the mystery of the Amazon. There is a powerful force of the land in his fantastic music. Many kinds of music involve me and give me peace. North American blues, Brazilian samba, Cape Verdean *morna*. The Cape Verdean *morna* is the Brazilian *modinha*, popular at the beginning of the century. When I went to Cape Verde for the first time and I heard the *mornas*, I was nostalgic for Brazil, especially for the time when the *modinha* was popular, a time I, myself, did not experience, but I know through music. Popular music fascinates me also, but classical music is classic, I suppose, because it is people-based.

I love to read. And I love to write, even though it is not easy for me to write. For me, writing is always a difficult but tasteful exercise. I also love ordinary things like sports, especially soccer. I love the sea, the beaches. And I love to take walks on the beach and sunbathe in the tropical sun. I like to walk in big cities. New York relaxes me. I like to be lost in the center of great cities. I sometimes do not feel so good when I feel lost in small communities.

I love to receive letters. I receive a lot of letters and I try to answer them with the help of a good friend. Occasionally I think I should send a letter to the world, asking people *not* to write because it is not easy for me to answer all of my letters. But my friend has volunteered to help me, and she has been very helpful.

I love children. I may be wrong, but I think children also love me a lot. Not just my grandchildren, who obviously know I am their grandfather, but children on the street. In Europe they used to call me Santa Claus on Christmas Eve, in Brazil also, because of my white beard. They come running to me on the streets. Sometimes I ask myself why. I guess I don't scare them!

When I was twenty-three years old and newly married I began to discover, but I was not always able to state explictly, that the only way we can stay alive, alert, and be true philosophers is never to let the child within us die. Society pressures us to kill this child, but we must resist, because when we kill the child within us, we kill ourselves. We wither and age before our time. Today I am sixty-two years old but I often feel ten or twenty years old. When I climb five flights of stairs my body lets me know my age, but what is inside my old body is deeply alive, simply because I preserve the child within me. I also think my body is youthful and as alive as this child who I once was and continue to be, this child who leads me to love life so much.

I feel my incompleteness inside me, at the biological, affective, criticial, and intellectual levels, an incompleteness that pushes me constantly, curiously, and lovingly toward other people and the world, searching for solidarity and transcendence of solitude. All of this implies wanting to love, a capacity for love that people must create in themselves. This capacity increases to the degree that one loves; it diminishes when one is afraid to love. Of course, in our society it is not easy to love, because we derive much of our happiness from sadness; that is, very often for us to feel happy, others must be sad. Under these circumstances it is difficult to love, but it is necessary to do so.

I love simple things, common, everyday places. I hate sophisticated, snobbish gatherings where people do not know what to do with their hands: should you put them on the armchair, fiddle with your necktie, your beard? Not knowing what to do with your hands is a sign of being uncomfortable. I detest this kind of gathering. I love to be comfortable.

I love to know that I love Elza. We have been married and experiencing each other's love for forty years. I love to be with her and with my children. I love being a father. I never found anything wrong with being a father. As a young man I thought living and sleeping with a woman (out of which come other people, unasked, and on whom the world depends) might interrupt my intellectual life. If this were so, I still would have preferred my life with Elza and my children to my intellectual life. But since I never found my family and my intellectual lives to be incompatible, I was able to have a family and write at the same time. My family did not interfere with my writing, and my writing did not interfere with my love for my family. This is why I write with great love and why I love to write.

Macedo: *What final advice do you have for readers?*

Freire: I can offer no specific advice, but here are a few brotherly suggestions. First, start rereading this book. Your second reading should be far more critical than the first. I suggest this not only for this book but for all your reading.

Whether it be a raindrop (a raindrop that was about to fall but froze, giving birth to a beautiful icicle), be it a bird that sings, a bus that runs, a violent person on the street, be it a sentence in the newspaper, a political speech, a lover's rejection, be it anything, we must adopt a critical view, that of the person who questions, who doubts, who investigates, and who wants to illuminate the very life we live.

My suggestion is that we capture our daily alienation, the alienation of our routine, of repeating things bureaucratically, of doing the same thing every day at ten o'clock, for example, because "it has to be done" and we never question why. We should take our lives into our own hands and begin to exercise control. We should try to stand up to, and get out from under time

In these complex societies we sometimes find ourselves living very much submerged in time, without critical and dynamic appreciation of history, as if history were flying over us, commanding and relentlessly regulating our lives. This is a fatalism that immobilizes, sufffocates, and eventually kills us. History is nothing like this. History has no power. As Marx has said, history does not command us, history is made by us. History makes us while we make it. Again, my suggestion is that we attempt to emerge from this alienating daily routine that repeats itself. Let's try to understand life, not necessarily as the daily repetition of things, but as an effort to create and re-create, and as an effort to rebel, as well. Let's take our alienation into our own hands and ask, "Why?" "Does it have to be this way?" I do not think so. We need to be subjects of history, even if we cannot totally stop being objects of history. And to be subjects, we need unquestionably to claim history critically. As active participants and real subjects, we can make history only when we are continually critical of our very lives.

Index

RELATED BOOKS

Theory and Resistance in Education
A Pedagogy for the Opposition
Henry A. Giroux
Foreword by Paulo Freire • Introduction by Stanley Aronowitz

"A creative experience . . . . It should be read by everyone interested in education, social theory, and critical practice."   *—Paulo Freire*

"Perhaps the most important book (and most regenerating to the pedagogic struggle) that I've read since 1975. Even the most complex sections glint and gleam with brilliance."   *—Jonathan Kozol*

"It marks a significant moment in the development of a radical theory of education."   *—Michael Ryan*, Curriculum Inquiry

Education Under Siege
The Conservative, Liberal, and Radical Debate over Schooling
Stanley Aronowitz and Henry A. Giroux

The Authors develop radically new insights into the possibilities for educators to address the nature of learning and the purpose of schooling. This visionary book should be read by every student, educator, and citizen concerned with a creative new approach to education, and its ultimate goal—liberation.

The Crisis in Historical Materialism
Class, Politics and Culture in Marxist Theory
Stanley Aronowitz

"A *tour de force* and necessary reading for anyone interested in Marxism, Continental philosophy, or contemporary American life."
—Cornel West, The Village Voice

Bergin & Garvey Publishers. 670 Amherst Road. S. Hadley, Massachusetts 01075

NOTES

1. Henry Giroux, author of *Theory & Resistance in Education*, 1983 and co-author of *Education Under Siege*, 1985.

2. Martin Carnoy, author most recently of *The State of Political Theory*, 1984; and Ann Berthoff, author of *Forming/Thinking/Writing: The Composing Imagination*, 1978 and *Reclaiming the Imagination: Philosophical Perspectives for Writers and Teachers of Writing*, 1984.

3. Agnes Heller, author of *The Theory of Need in Marx*, 1976 and *A Theory of History*, 1982.